THE SAME AS CHRIST JESUS
GOSPEL AND TYPE

PETER MALONE

The Same as Christ Jesus

Gospel and Type

ST PAULS

ST PAULS Publishing
187 Battersea Bridge Road
London SW11 3AS, UK

Copyright © ST PAULS 2000

ISBN 085439 592 X

Australian edition published by
ST PAULS PUBLICATIONS – Society of St Paul
60-70 Broughton Road, PO Box 906, Strathfield NSW 2135
www.stpauls.com.au

ISBN 1 876295 34 1

Set by TuKan DTP, Fareham, UK
Produced in the EC
Printed by Interprint Ltd., Marsa, Malta

ST PAULS is an activity of the priests and brothers
of the Society of St Paul who proclaim the Gospel
through the media of social communication

Contents

Introduction	7
A Personal Gospel and Type Journey	9
Mark's Gospel	25
Prelude to Jesus' Public Ministry	25
Disciples and Ministers	28
Jesus the Teacher	33
Jesus in Action	35
Matthew's Gospel	41
The Jewish Background	41
Fulfilment Texts	42
Apocalyptic Literature	44
Structure of the Gospel	46
The Law	48
'No Frills' Language	49
Challenge before Harmony	51
Parables of Justice	53
Jesus and Encounters	54
Women in Matthew's Gospel	56
Luke's Gospel	59
Style and Structure	60
Prologue to Ministry: The Infancy Narratives	61
Jesus' Encounters	64
Jesus' Parables	67
Emmaus	73

John's Gospel   75
    The Johannine Community   75
    High Christology   76
    Structure   77
    John and the Jewish Scriptures   78
    Signs and Wonders   82
    Johannine Theology   83
    Jesus' Hour   86
    Resurrection Stories   90

Jesus, our Spirituality and Type   93

Matthew's Jesus   97

Mark's Jesus   103

Luke's Jesus   109

John's Jesus   115

Gospels and Temperament   121

'The Custodian', SJ and Matthew's Gospel   123

'The Artisan', SP and Mark's Gospel   125

'The Idealist', NF and Luke's Gospel   127

'The Visionary', NT and John's Gospel   131

Finally   133

Appendix: The Myers Briggs Type Indicator   135

Bibliography   143

Introduction

'The same as Christ Jesus...'. It is surprising that these striking words of Paul to the Philippians are not quoted more often. They offer a wonderful briefing for the Christian life, for discipleship, the following of Jesus Christ:

> If our life in Christ means anything to you, if love can persuade at all, or the Spirit that we have in common, or any tenderness and sympathy, then be united in your convictions and united in your love, with a common purpose and a common mind. That is the one thing that would make me completely happy. There must be no competition among you, no conceit; but everybody is to be self-effacing. Always consider the other person to be better than yourself, so that nobody thinks of their own interests first but everybody thinks of other people's interests instead (Phil 2:1-4).

Then, before Paul quotes an early Christian hymn to Jesus' emptying himself, so to speak, of his divine life in order to live our human lives with us and like us, becoming as we are, there is one brief verse (v.5) which could be Paul's exhortation of all time:

> In your minds you must be the same as Christ Jesus.

In our minds, in our hearts, we are to be the same as Jesus who lived our human lives with us. How do we respond to this urgent invitation of Paul? How can we? What is it like in my limited yet unique experience to be 'the same as Christ Jesus'?

One of the ways that I have found most helpful for more than twenty years is through the insights and the affirmation I have experienced through what is known as Psychological Type.

And this means...?

A Personal Gospel and Type Journey

Call it providence, call it synchronicity, call it grace, but there are great blessings in being in a good place at the right time.

The place was Berkeley, California, the time was the autumn term, 1978. There were fourteen men and women from Australia studying or visiting at the Graduate Theological Union. (The discovery of Chicago and Boston for overseas studies was soon to come, in the 80s!) Then, and certainly in retrospect, it was an exciting time. Almost a decade had gone by since the campus unrest and demonstrations of the late 60s and students were now calmly riding bicycles or getting round on skateboards. Jane Fonda came to the University to speak, but she had already won an Oscar for 'Klute' and within six months was to win another for the post-Vietnam/war drama, 'Coming Home', so her speeches on justice had a different fervour from her actions and protests of the heady anti-war years.

But, although it was new and seemed at first just another self-help device, one of the stimulating things about Berkeley 1978 was a questionnaire that you could fill in, 'Form G', and learn something about your personality type. There was a hyphenated name associated with it, Myers-Briggs.

It's the same as it is with friends. You often remember when you met them and the immediate impact, but the rest of the getting-to-know-you-better process, the shared experiences and the growing intimacy, overshadow the detailed memory of what happened initially.

I remember Noel Davis, later the author of books of poetry, *Heart Gone Walkabout* and *Campfires of the Heart* telling me about another new word and process, the Enneagram, and about the Myers-Briggs form. It was a Sunday in late November, 1978. I inked in the circles, A or B, about whether I preferred justice or mercy, was the life of the party or not, preferred to speak or to write and 123 more questions. Noel used some grids to score the answers and informed me that I was an INFJ. It seemed something of a slogan or a catch-phrase at the time, but it is one of the pieces of information that has had most influence on my life. (At this stage there may be some readers who would like a little more background to the Myers Briggs Type Indicator either by way of introduction or by way of memory refresher. The appendix on the MBTI is offered as a briefing.)

These were the days before Isabel Myers' *Gifts Differing* was published. David Keirsey and Marilyn Bates's *Please Understand Me* was available only in galley form. But it was their description of an INFJ, which seemed uncannily perceptive and accurate, that led me into wanting to understand more about Type.

Many people, especially in religious circles, were ready for the introduction to Type in the 70s. It was an era of great interest in Jung. Once again, I cannot remember in much detail when I first became interested in Jung and dreams. We had studied a little of Freud, Jung and Adler in our seminary History of Philosophy course in the late 50s. We knew that the English Dominican priest, Victor White, had discussed religious and psychological issues with Jung.

In the 70s my ministry was in religious formation, in training students for priesthood and for life in a religious order. It was the age of process and self-development and, in the Catholic tradition, an age of renewal and re-shaping the style of ministry and community living. We were interested in spirituality and in the theology of religious experience which was being developed by my confrere, Frank Fletcher. So, Jung (or, at least, a smattering of Jung) and learning about some of his significant concepts became an important part of the quest for self-understanding and Jung's insights were used in counselling work.

Man and his Symbols, with Jung's article on dreams, the other articles by people like Marie Louise von Franz, the range of illustrations (and stills from movies) lured us into reflection on our dreams. We were on the verge of archetypes.

One of the other benefits of being in Berkeley in 1978 was the possibility of going to seminars at the Jung Centre in San Francisco. Within two weeks of arriving, I was able to attend a lecture by John Sanford, who had become something of a hero at that time with *The Kingdom Within* and *Healing and Wholeness*. He could speak as invigoratingly as he wrote. The lecture was the core of his book on animus and anima, *Invisible Partners*.

Another lively seminar considered symbols of evil. On the Sunday night it ended, I was staying at the De La Salle Brothers' community and sleeping in a basement visitors' room. I woke up suddenly at what turned out to be 3.00 am feeling a weight on my chest and stomach. I looked up and thought I saw a black cat sitting on me. Although usually prone to scepticism, I was surprised and alarmed. After I blinked, there was nothing to be seen. However, I turned on the light and there was the cat sitting on the mat. It then rushed up to the high window of the basement and scurried out. 'Oh, yes', said one of the Brothers, 'we should have mentioned it. If you leave your window open, the cat gets in.' This left my scepticism intact, but it reinforced my interest in synchronicity.

When it became clear that Isabel Myers and her mother, Katharine Briggs, were admirers of Jung, the Myers-Briggs Type Indicator seemed even more interesting. Its practical value was confirmed by a learning experience. Most of the fourteen Australians were pretty outgoing. They enjoyed meeting for dinners or parties. In fact, one sister who had worked in Papua New Guinea was an American and had been given a credit card by her father to use while she was studying. He regularly complained to her that she was not taking advantage of it often enough. So, off we went to the Napa Valley and other better than sundry destinations.

But I found the socialising rather draining. When I learned what Jung meant by extraversion and introversion and discovered that INFJ meant that I had a preference for introversion, I begged out one evening. But I was still feeling bad, because socialising seemed to be the right and expected thing to do. Next morning, nobody seemed in the least put out that I was not there. They did say it was a pity that I couldn't come because it had been a really great evening. But it had been a great evening for me, realising that I did not have to live up to false expectations that I had taken for granted. It was all right being introverted and acting that way.

Whatever it was, Myers Briggs seemed to be just right. Scepticism cautioned that it might just be another passing trend in self-help (soon to be 'New Age') resources, just a fad. And, of course, for many it has been, often superseded by a faddish use of the Enneagram; from enjoying being, for instance, a self-proclaimed ESFJ to being a self-proclaimed 3! But even the passing interest has helped a lot of people and can't simply be dismissed.

Myers Briggs' work helps to explain personality, not explain it away. It helps us to appreciate, not merely in terms of behaviour (which can be quite misleading) but in terms of our inner processes – how we tick! – how we function. We can understand better where we function best, in the outer world of action, people, events or in our inner world of thoughts, feelings, imagination, whether we are extraverts or introverts.

Since all of us function in the outer world, whether we are extraverts or not, we need to understand *how* we function there, whether we are decisive types or data-gathering types, whether we are Judgers and Perceivers.

But, how do we perceive best? Through the five senses and making contact with here and now reality and relishing this, Sensation? Or, going beyond the five senses to the realm of possibilities and hunches, Intuition?

And, how do we judge best, what criteria? Objective, logical and impersonal and just criteria, Thinking? Or more subjective, circumstantial and personalised and harmony fostering criteria, Feeling?

So far in this Type journey there has been no mention of Type and the Gospels. Once again, I cannot quite remember when I first found it useful to link Type theory with the Gospels. But, back in Melbourne in 1979, I continued work with the students who had joined the religious congregation to which belong, the Missionaries of the Sacred Heart. With Type in mind, I realised that the insights were invaluable in having the students name their characteristics and differences and in their realising where there was potential for clash and the need for conflict resolution.

I also found that I had been working well for many years with a colleague who was INFP and most congenial. I discovered as well why I had never noticed cobwebs around a cloister which the Vocations Recruiter invariably commented on during his visits. Of course, he was ISFJ. I think this call to notice cobwebs was the first of many Perception challenges I failed and continue, despite best efforts, to fail.

But it was the patterns of prayer of the students and their response to the Gospels and the person of Jesus that alerted me to the religious dimension of Type. Later, when I was to read in Chester Michael's *Prayer and Temperament* that

INFJs disliked regular and repetitive prayer, it was another liberation. (The hard part is that this is the challenge to my shadow and a means to wholeness, something I can assent to in Thinking-function faith, but still find it difficult to embrace with Feeling-function faith.)

And the Gospels. I am not sure when Margaret Dwyer alerted me to aspects of prayer and the Gospels. She was later to publish *Wake up the Sun* with her own approach and questionnaire to facilitate discovery of Type. (This was later revised and reprinted in two books, the first, *No Light without Shadow*, with her introduction to Type, the second with applications of Type to spirituality.) Margaret was in Berkeley in 1978. On her return to Australia and appointment to the Catholic Education Office in Melbourne, she introduced Myers Briggs seminars, one of the first people in pioneering Type and its use in Australia. She also led seminars developing the Type insights into prayer.

Her studies in the US had included studying prayer and Type and she spent some time at a Jesuit retreat-house at Wernersville, Pa. By 1983, some of those associated with the retreat-house published a book on prayer and Type, based on their spiritual direction of retreatants, including using the retreatant's awareness of their own Type. The book was *From Image to Likeness – A Jungian Path in the Gospel Journey*. The authors were W. Harold Grant, Magdala Thompson and Thomas E. Clarke. It is still one of the best books on prayer and Type.

At Wernersville, one of the perceptions was that each of the four Gospels seemed to be permeated by one of the four Jungian functions. As always, there is a great danger in generalising and in labelling. (The negative overtones of 'labelling' tend to be stressed – confining people within narrow headings and definitions – while the positive overtones of a label as a means to identifying and highlighting a particular aspect and encouraging people to range widely within that aspect tend to be downplayed or ignored.) However, the arresting point was made that Mark's Gospel seems to be particularly Sensate, Matthew's Gospel rather more Thinking-toned while Luke's was more Feeling-toned. John's Gospel seemed more Intuitive.

The connection for me was a memory that there used to be a section of the *Introduction to the New Testament* course which spoke of the traditional descriptions of the Gospels. It had been said for centuries, without benefit of Jung or Type, that Mark's Gospel was quite detailed and vivid. It was said that it was like an 'eye-witness' Gospel and one of the most popular explanations suggested was that Mark acted as a secretary for the apostle, Peter, and that he was really writing down the accurate picture of the events of Jesus' life as remembered and dictated by Peter. It was really Peter's Gospel.

All commentators except the most fundamentalist acknowledge that this description is based on a limited understanding of the formation of the Gospel tradition, of the processes of remembering and preaching by many of Jesus' disciples rather than by an individual, that it is more accurate to describe the Gospel as compiled and edited by 'the Markan community'.

However, the 'eye-witness' Gospel seemed to me to be a strongly Sensate description. In fact, one of the exercises in looking at the Synoptic Gospels during the New Testament course was to place the accounts of some of the events common to Matthew, Mark and Luke alongside each other and spot the differences. The case in point that I remember from classes is that of Jesus going to the house of Jairus to raise his little daughter to life and his being interrupted on the way by the woman with the haemorrhage, the woman who touched his cloak. The Markan version is much longer than that of Matthew or of Luke. There is more detail of the woman's illness, Jesus' response and of the visit to Jairus' house and what Jesus did there in Mark 5:21-43, compared with Matthew 9:18-26 and Luke 8:40-56 – 23 Markan verses to Matthew's 9 and Luke's 17).

What of the other Gospels and Type?

The core of Matthew's Gospel was frequently spoken of in the tradition as being a collection of the sayings of Jesus, the teachings of Jesus. When one notices, especially, that the people who listened to Jesus' Sermon on the Mount (Mt 5-7) were described as being amazed at his teaching because he spoke with 'authority', then it is not a difficult move to seeing Matthew's Gospel as a Thinking-function Gospel. The orderly structure of the Gospel reinforces this perception.

On the other hand, there has been constant reference to Luke's Gospel as the Gospel of compassion. Because of the detailed Infancy Narratives in Luke 1-2, Luke was considered by some to have received his information from Mary, the mother of Jesus. Again, there is a stronger presence of women in Luke's Gospel than in the others. There were also the old traditions that Luke was a painter as well as a doctor and these qualifications helped him produce this compassionate Gospel, a Feeling-function Gospel. Once again, this interpretation of Luke is based on a limited understanding of the Gospel as the work of one person.

This, of course, leaves only John and Intuition. John's Gospel has always been considered 'mystical'. It is rarely thought of as an eye-witness account although there are some well-remembered details from Cana (ch. 2), the story of the woman at the well (ch. 4) and from the raising of Lazarus from the dead (ch. 11). Rather, it is the discourses of Jesus that form the bulk of John's Gospel, more intuitive reflections on the meaning of who Jesus was and on his union with the Father. There seems to be little difficulty in considering John's as an Intuitive-function Gospel.

Theologians, when speaking of the understanding of the

humanity and the divinity of Jesus, suggest that there are two approaches. They are called High Christology and Low Christology. What they mean by 'High Christology' is that the divinity of Jesus is considered first and the humanity is understood in the light of the divinity. It is a Christology 'from above'. So, for the Gospel accounts, it is reading the divinity (which, in fact, was only later understood by the disciples) back into the story of Jesus of Nazareth. In some of the Gospel stories, the narrative is about Jesus but the text will refer to him as 'the Lord'. The raising of the son of the widow of Nain (Lk 7:11-17) has this usage as has the story of the visit to Martha and Mary (Lk 10:39-42) where Mary sits 'at the Lord's feet'.

By way of contrast, the 'Low Christology' means that the humanity of Jesus is of primary consideration. It is a Christology 'from below'. Only later does the consideration of the divinity emerge. The tradition has been that the Synoptic Gospels have been written from the Low Christology perspective. They start with Jesus of Nazareth and, as the Gospel progresses, a deeper understanding of Jesus emerges leading to an understanding of him as divine. John's Gospel was written from the perspective of a High Christology. It begins that way in the first verse of the prologue, that the Word was not only with God, but was God.

This can highlight how Mark and John contrast. Mark's Gospel, the Sensate Gospel, works from the detail of the words and actions of Jesus of Nazareth. It is anchored in the present Sensate reality. One can move from this Low Christology to more Intuitive understandings of Jesus as both human and divine. On the other hand, John's Gospel offers many possibilities of intuitive understanding of the complex person of Jesus, both human and divine. If one wants to appreciate the reality of the incarnation, one must move towards the literally mundane ('of this world') details of Jesus' words and actions.

St Irenaeus, c.130–c.200 AD, who is best remembered for his statement that the glory of God is the human person fully alive, also said that it was most appropriate that there were four (and only four) canonical Gospels. He appealed to the fact that there were the four points of the compass and that four winds could blow from these directions. This is more than a touch archetypal. But it suggests that it is appropriate that there be four Gospels.

There seems also to be a providence, some synchronicity that the Gospels can be linked to each of the four Type functions. Paul, in his first letter to the Corinthians, (9:22-23), says that in his preaching 'he became all things to all people for the sake of the Gospel and to have a share in its blessings'. It means that the Good News was proclaimed in such a way that it could be appreciated by all Types. There were all Types in each of the early Christian communities but what seems to have emerged is that each of the four Gospel communities perceived Jesus in a particular way and that, together, this four Gospel portrait is of a Jesus who is all things to all people.

John Sanford, in looking at Type's basic attitudes and functions, studies the four Gospels and finds that Jesus is portrayed substantially as living out of all of them. (*The Kingdom Within: a Study of the Inner Meaning of Jesus' Sayings*, Lippincott, Philadelphia, 1970.) There are sufficiently strong Gospel passages that show Jesus as both Introvert and Extravert, both Judging and Perceiving, both Sensing and Intuitive, both Thinking and Feeling. Sanford uses the word 'ambivert' to describe Jesus. Another way of describing the Jesus of the Gospels is 'omnivert'.

Some personal experiences reinforced this approach to the Gospels for me.

In the 70s, British actor Alec McCowan appeared on stage reciting the Gospel of Mark. With fifteen chapters, it is the shortest of the Gospels. It is not such a protracted piece for a theatrical experience. But, the point is that, with its eye-witness qualities, it appeals to the broadest audience sensibilities and provides them with ample detail to help them imagine Jesus and the encounters and events of his life and death.

I also came to realise that, with students who were not familiar with the Gospels and were, indeed, somewhat intimidated by the prospect of reading and re-reading them, often the Gospel of Mark was just what they needed, especially with those who identified with the Sensing function.

On the other hand, Type theory can be sabotaged by reality. Ask any group of people with whom you are trying to verify these theories, about their favourite Gospel after they have been studying John with an expert lecturer. The answer is, unanimously, John! Frank Moloney, one of Australia's and the world's leading experts on John has ruined my research many a time.

Another experience also highlighted the Type response to the Gospels and, indeed, to the Jesus of the Gospels: days of retreat or recollection for men. For a cross-section of men from a parish, it seems best to start with a talk based on Matthew's Gospel. You can almost see the level-headed Thinking men (who collect and count the collections, who organise working bees) nodding their heads in agreement with a practical down-to-earth Jesus, whose 'yes' is 'yes' and whose 'no' is 'no'. The Golden Rule of doing to others as you would have others do to you makes perfect sense.

But, as the day goes on, it is worth moving to a Lukan Jesus.

The parable of the Prodigal Son has Jesus at his storytelling and empathetic best and the men can identify with it. At the end of a day, I have been with a man weeping, telling me the story of his harshness to his son, cutting him off and not being able to communicate with him anymore.

It seemed that if we had started with the Feeling, Lukan Jesus, it might have been too emotional for the men and, therefore, alienating. But, starting with a credible Thinking Jesus that the men could identify with and then moving with them to the challenge of the Feeling Jesus, is a movement of grace that the men can respond to and respond more deeply than we could have anticipated.

These experiences reinforced the desire to relate Type to the Gospels and the practical applications of these insights to personal spirituality.

But another direction opened up in the mid-80s. With my work in film reviewing and writing, I found that I was noticing how characters in films were dramatising aspects of Type. It became clear that when a writer and director (even without benefit of Jung and Isabel Myers) had insights into human nature, their portraits could be looked at in terms of Type. Perhaps the first example did not indicate the fulfilment of the promise of Type-watching at the movies. It was Michael Douglas as a judge in the 1984 movie, 'The Star Chamber', where a group of judges who resented criminals being let free from the courts because of mis-trials or the persuasive speeches of shrewd lawyers took to executing the criminals themselves. The issues of justice were presented in a very clear-cut way, objectively, determinedly, concretely. It seemed that I was looking at an ISTJ situation with some ISTJ characters.

Encouraged by this, I thought it might be a good idea to find sixteen characters who dramatised convincingly each of the sixteen Myers Briggs Types. The discovery this time was that it is easy to dramatise extraverts; it is easy to dramatise sensates; it is easy to dramatise thinkers and feelers. But it is harder to dramatise introverts and even harder to dramatise intuitives. The practical conclusion was that it is very difficult to find introverted intuitives up there on the screen, INFJ and INTJ being the hardest of all (although Woody Allen movies tend to provide examples).

While re-watching Pier Paolo Pasolini's 1964 'Gospel According to Matthew', I realised that Jesus was being portrayed in a particular way, a way that did not entirely appeal to me. The INTJ that I needed was leaping (no, that is hardly an INTJ word) from the screen at me. This Pasolini Jesus ended up as the INTJ chapter of a little book considering 16 characters from the 16 Types and, by using the text and texture of the movie, analyse their type development throughout the film. Not my idea, perhaps a touch too flamboyant for INFJ sensibility, but the book was called, *Myers Briggs Goes to the Movies*!

It was time to start examining how Jesus had been presented on screen in Type terms. There seemed to be several Sensate portrayals of Jesus, including 'King of Kings'. Pasolini had provided an obviously Thinking function Jesus in his 'Gospel According to Matthew'. This contrasted forcefully with Zeffirelli's 'Jesus of Nazareth', a Feeling Function Jesus. Once again, it took some time to find an Intuitive portrayal of Jesus but, in the early 90s, audiences were surprised by Denys Arcand's 'Jesus of Montreal'. Pasolini's and Arcand's Jesus-figures were introverted. If you want a more markedly extraverted Jesus, then Martin Scorsese's 'Last Temptation of Christ' is the movie. It is the movie where Jesus most enjoys the wedding feast at Cana. He does some eating, drinking and dancing before he does his miraculous good deed in turning water into wine.

During the 90s, there has been a great deal more writing about Type and spirituality. I have learned a great deal in seminars on prayer and spirituality as well as using film clips of the Jesus-movies to illustrate Gospel and Type. Most of the books are about prayer and reflections on the Gospels. They explain and illustrate the connections between prayer and the various functions. *From Image to Likeness* has sections on Jesus and Type and prayer exercises based on the Gospels in each of its major chapters Type. They are written in such a way that everybody can read each chapter with profit. I am affirmed when I read the chapter on Intuiting: Hope (with the tellingly ironic sub-title 'Eye has not seen') and see Jesus portrayed as 'Prophet, Dreamer, Fool' and where the Gospel reference in the exercises is only to John. I am challenged by the chapter on Sensing: Simplicity (and sometimes long for 'The Gift to be Simple') where Jesus is referred to as 'Model of Sensing/Simplicity', Servant, with emphasis on his example, touch, suffering and the main Gospel references are to Mark.

Some authors have continued the speculations of John Sanford and have moved away from his conclusion that Jesus is ambivert. Otto Kroeger and Roy M. Oswald, in *Personality Type and Religious Leadership* (p.52), 'suspect that Jesus was an INFP or an INFJ' (which I initially warmed to! but it is a bit dangerous and misleading to speculate too specifically). Using Temperament Theory, they suggest in chapter 6, *Temperaments and the Pastoral Role*, that the Gospel most favoured by SPs would be Mark, by SJs Matthew, by NTs John and by NFs Luke.

Terence Duniho, in his *Wholeness Lies Within – 16 Natural Paths to Spirituality*, has two chapters on the Gospels. He rejects the ambivert theory. He says that the incarnation means that Jesus was a human being and, therefore, would have developed and manifested a particular type. While he acknowledges that the Gospels are not the work of one author but rather of a community, he looks at the four Gospels, conflating the episodes into a developmental biography of Jesus and, by a process of elimination, draws the conclusion that the Gospels present Jesus as an ENTP. This approach tends to read stylised texts as naturalistic texts and to assume that the accounts heard by the Gospel community and filtered through their response is naturalistically accurate.

In 1997, British Anglican priest and Professor of Theology in Wales, Leslie J. Francis, published *Personality Type and Scripture – Exploring Mark's Gospel*. This book takes the approach that Mark's Gospel is, rightly, for all readers. He takes the Sunday Gospel readings from the Lectionary and offers for each a Sensate interpretation, an Intuitive interpretation, a Feeling interpretation and a Thinking interpretation. He himself is INTJ.

His first example is the preaching of John the Baptist (Mk1:1-8). After a brief explanation of the context of the passage, he urges sensates to listen to the stillness of the wilderness and then hear the voice, imagine the scroll with the text of Isaiah quoted, see what is happening at the Jordan. For the intuitives, he highlights the words 'prepare' and 'repent' and urges them to go on a thematic journey ranging from Advent to Easter, to sacraments of confirmation and communion. Meanwhile, the feelers are stepping into John's sandals to share the experience of being baptised, appreciating his mission and being challenged in their own. Finally, the thinkers are urged to do some exegetical reflection on the nature of the book, its authorship and clarifying that Exodus 23 is also being incorporated into the quotation from Isaiah 40 so that John the Baptist's mission makes sense.

This book appreciates the different approaches to the Gospels but goes back to the Wernersville suggestions, confirmed by the popular tradition of the Church, of seeing Mark's as the Sensate Gospel, Matthew's as the Thinking Gospel, Luke's as the Feeling Gospel, John's as the Intuitive Gospel. This approach is not meant to be labelling and constricting. Rather, it opens up a way into the richness of each of the Gospel portraits of Jesus.

And that seems to be the way to go: an exploration of each Gospel and its Type portrait of Jesus. I will try to write in a style appropriate to each function when considering each

Gospel: the narration of events in order in Mark with an attention to their sensate detail; a clear and objective presentation of the issues and style of Matthew; a more personalised portrait of the person of Jesus, his message, his contacts and relationships in Luke; the exploration of the signs and wonders dramatised in John's Gospel, permeated with the reflections and meditation of the discourses of Jesus.

Mark's Gospel

It is generally agreed that the Gospel of Mark is the earliest Gospel, the core Gospel. Matthew and Luke seem to use it as the centre of their Gospels, adding their own particular material and shaping it according to the interests of their communities, Jewish interests, Graeco-Roman interests.

Mark was named second in the listing of Matthew, Mark, Luke and John. The 'sayings' of Jesus that are at the core of Matthew may have been an original tradition. But the Gospel as both the announcing of the Good News of the Kingdom and as the journey of Jesus from his earliest ministry to his death and resurrection, is what we understand now as a Gospel.

Mark's Gospel was often referred to in the tradition as the 'eye-witness' Gospel. Mark was thought to be Peter's secretary and, in writing his Gospel, he used the accounts that Peter gave in his preaching and in his reminiscences. Mark's was considered to be a vivid Gospel, offering a detailed portrait of Jesus. One could call it a Sensate Gospel.

Making our way through this Gospel in an orderly, chronological way, we can develop our understanding of Jesus and his message, his words and his actions.

Prelude to Jesus' Public Ministry

The opening of the Gospel states quite clearly the aim of this book, indicating the theological and spiritual perspective of the account of Jesus' ministry collected by the Markan community: 'The beginning of the Good News about Jesus Christ the Son of God'. The 'beginning' of this verse reminds us of the opening of the Jewish Scriptures in

Genesis, 'In the beginning...'. This is the beginning of the new covenant.

Mark also uses the word 'Gospel' which has always been used to describe the books of Matthew, Mark, Luke and John. But, basically, it means the Good News of Jesus himself and his preaching of repentance and the coming of God's reign. We use the phrase, 'to preach the Gospel', 'to live according to the Gospel'.

Jesus is called the Son of God. This is not what later generations would call a claim for the divinity of Jesus. Rather, Jesus, in the Gospel of Mark, is presented as Jesus of Nazareth, a graced human being who is portrayed in a very human way. As the Gospel progresses, Jesus' relationship with God emerges as stronger than what is usual even for prophets and significant religious figures. Later generations would understand Jesus as both human and divine. But, in Mark's Gospel, while readers would appreciate the post-resurrection knowledge of Jesus' divinity inherent in the Gospel, the presentation of Jesus is from a perspective that is referred to as 'Low Christology', from humanity to divinity, 'from below' so to speak.

This reinforces the Sensate character of the Gospel. Jesus is observed in his present moment, in the concrete situations in which he finds himself. His development is observed, not anticipated.

With the preaching of John the Baptist, the baptism of Jesus and the temptation in the wilderness, the Gospel introduces Jesus (1:1-13). Scripture scholar Raymond Brown once suggested that a way of considering these stories is to compare them to a triptych, one of those medieval altar-pieces below the table and facing the congregation. A triptych is one work of art. But it is made up of three separate pictures. Each can be looked at in itself. But each flows into the other and can be looked at as a whole.

This Markan triptych consists of a picture of John the Baptist, introduced by a quotation from the book of Isaiah which sets the tone and suggests that the coming of Jesus is as joyful and as comforting an event as the return of the Jews from their fifty years of exile in Babylon (587-537 BC) and starting their community afresh. John, who is described vividly as wearing a garment of camel-skin and eating wild locusts, urges the confessing of sin and a baptism of repentance in the river Jordan. He also announces the coming of a preacher and baptiser who is greater than he. John baptises with water. The new preacher will baptise with the spirit of God. (The prophet Ezekiel in speaking of cleansing and purifying water had said that this water was filled with God's Spirit (36:24-28).

The second picture of the triptych centres on Jesus himself. Jesus arrives. He is baptised by John in the Jordan. Wonderful signs accompany the baptism: a sundering of the heavens, God's Spirit resting on Jesus in the form of a dove, a voice proclaiming that Jesus is the true servant of God. The voice is quoting the first servant song from the book of Isaiah where the servant is singled out, the spirit rests on him and he is called 'beloved' as he begins his ministry, gently, as a light to the nations and a covenant of the people (42:1-6).

Thus announced and established as a prophet, Jesus is led into the desert by the spirit of God. This is the third picture of the triptych. For forty days Jesus is tested by Satan. The references are to the forty years that the people of Israel wandered the desert, often unfaithful to the covenant, before entering into the promised land as well as to the angel in God's court who was what we might now call 'the devil's advocate', the Satan who put Job, who remained faithful to God, to the test. (It was later that the Satan took on our familiar diabolical overtones.) Where Israel of old failed, Jesus succeeds in his temptation and testing and, as the psalms often say, he was protected by God's messengers, the angels.

Jesus' preparation for his ministry is now complete.

Disciples and Ministers

The Gospel makes it clear that John the Baptist is arrested by Herod and Jesus begins his ministry. Later, in 6:17-29, Mark will describe the situation in Herod's court and the dance of the daughter of Herodias which led to John's execution.

Jesus announces the good news of the kingdom (1:14-15) and immediately calls his first disciples. They are actually fishing at the time of Jesus' call and the response is instant. They leave Zebedee and the other men in the boat and go.

But the introduction of Jesus to the people is through miracles. Those familiar with the prophet Isaiah would know that the time of God's special coming would be marked by signs:

> Then the eyes of the blind shall be opened,
> the ears of the deaf unsealed,
> then the lame shall leap like a deer
> and the tongues of the dumb shout for joy (35:5-6).

The first miracle in Mark (1:21-28) occurs after Jesus has been teaching in a synagogue and the people contrast his teaching with that of their religious leaders. They see Jesus teaching with authority, with authenticity and conviction. A demonically-possessed man is present and calls out, identifying Jesus in messianic terms, 'the Holy One of God', and shouting against Jesus' confrontation of the spirits of evil. Jesus rebukes him and commands his silence. He also orders the unclean spirit to leave the man. The man convulses, the evil spirit coming out of him, and is healed. Along with the authoritative teaching, this impresses the crowds and Jesus is talked about everywhere.

Jesus cures Peter's mother-in-law and many others, but the impressive story in this early part of the Gospel is the cure of the leper. It reveals something of Jesus' personality and his dealings with people.

The narrative (1:40-45) begins with the leper's coming to Jesus. This, of course, should never have happened. According to the prescriptions of the law, the leper should have remained outside the towns: a leper 'must wear his clothing torn and his hair disordered; he must shield his upper lip and cry, 'Unclean, unclean'. As long as the disease lasts he must be unclean; he must live outside the camp' (Lev 13:45-46). Lepers in ancient times were the literally marginalised.

Jesus and his reputation meant that the leper had the confidence to break the law. And Jesus allowed him to break it. He not only let him approach, he received him sympathetically. The leper pleads his cause on his knees and appeals to Jesus personally, 'If you want to, you can cure me.' Mark begins to reveal more about Jesus. Jesus is touched. He is moved with compassion. Not only is he willing to heal the leper, 'Of course I want to. Be cured!', but he, who has been emotionally touched by the leper, physically touches him. In a significant gesture, he stretches out his hand and touches the leper. This will be a characteristic of the Jesus of Mark. He touches people. It is a cogent reminder of the Sensate nature of the portrait of Jesus.

However, once the leper is healed, Jesus' tone of voice changes. He sounds more stern. He immediately sends the healed man away and orders him to fulfil the law of sacrifice prescribed for recovery.

This sternness of Jesus may at first sound surprising. But we can note Jesus' differing attitudes towards law in this story. When the issue is one concerning Jesus himself, he is freer in his interpretation of the law. He allows the leper to break through the restrictions and come close to him. However, when the issue concerns the rights of others, he is strict and ·strict for their protection. He wants the healed man to be able to find his place back in the community. This requires adherence to the letter of the law and the fulfilment of the Mosaic obligations. It is for the good of the healed man.

In the next chapter (2:23-28), Jesus will be quite clear on the nature of the law. In the episode of the disciples eating the ears of corn during their Sabbath walk in the fields and being rebuked for defiling the Sabbath, Jesus gives an example of a broad interpretation of law. David and his followers were starving and went into the House of God and ate loaves reserved for the priests. Jesus' conclusion from this experience is to declare that he is Master of the Sabbath. He gives his followers a profoundly simple principle for interpreting law: 'the Sabbath was made for people, not people for the Sabbath.'

However, there is still another point to be found in the story of the healing of the leper. One might argue that Jesus at the beginning of his ministry is a touch inexperienced and a touch naive. He actually 'sternly ordered him: Mind you say nothing to anyone'! If ever there was an impossible command given to someone who has had a life-changing experience, it is this. And, of course, the man cannot help himself and talks about his healing everywhere. The crowds throng. Mark's Gospel states that Jesus could not go into the towns but had to stay in places where nobody lived. Preachers have usually told us that Jesus was not yet ready for the crowds and avoided them. However, what is often overlooked is that Jesus had become a leper. In his compassionate touching of the leper, Jesus became unclean, he was technically a leper. Regulations required him to stay in a self-imposed quarantine for thirty days. If then there were no signs of the disease, Jesus could continue his life as normal.

But it does mean that, for this time, Jesus was a leper, unclean, required to tear his clothes, dishevel his hair, not use his own name, but identify himself as he called out from the margins, 'Unclean'.

Early in his ministry, Jesus is spoken of as a man of prayer, a man who spent time with God his Father, 'in the morning, long before dawn, he got up and left the house, and went off to a lonely place and prayed there' (1:35).

But he was not left in peace for long and he began his preaching journeys. 'Let us go elsewhere, to the neighbouring country towns, so that I can preach there too, because that is why I came.' And he went all through Galilee, preaching in their synagogues and casting out devils' (1:38-39).

But Jesus' miracles also made him aware of the relationship between physical illness and sinfulness; illness, not as a consequence of sin but, rather, illness and the need for healing as a powerful image of sin and the need for forgiveness. He portrays this quite dramatically in the healing of the paralytic (2:1-12). The story is important and is found in both Matthew's and Luke's Gospels. In Matthew it is presented in a straightforward way, the paralytic simply being brought before Jesus. In Luke there is a touch more drama. Jesus is crowded in so they have to let the paralytic through the roof down in front of Jesus.

In Mark, we get a sense of the drama unfolding before our eyes. After Jesus heals the leper, he returns, some time later, to Capernaum 'and word went round that he was back'. The place filled. 'So many people collected that there was no room left, even in front of the door.' Then a group with the paralytic 'carried by four men' arrives. 'But as the crowd made it impossible to get the man to Jesus, they stripped the roof over the place where Jesus was; and when they had made an opening, they lowered the stretcher on which the paralytic lay.' (It is descriptions like this that led readers to think of Mark's as the eye-witness Gospel, the Sensate Gospel.)

But Jesus offers the paralytic forgiveness of his sins because he had seen his and his companions' faith. Some of the religious leaders and the scribes are taken aback and consider this blasphemy, 'Who can forgive sins but God?' Jesus now has a touch of the intuitive. 'Inwardly aware that this was what they were thinking', he challenges them on which is easier to say, 'I forgive you' or 'Be healed'. He says he wants to prove to them that his authority is to forgive sins. He heals the paralytic. While Matthew simply says the man got up and went home, Mark has him getting up, picking up his stretcher at once and walking out in front of everyone. They were all astounded and praised God, 'we have never seen anything like this'.

This theme of forgiveness is continued in the succeeding stories. The tax-collector, Levi, sitting by the customs house is called to be an apostle. He later gives a dinner and Jesus and his disciples are present. A number of tax collectors and sinners were also there, 'for there were many of them among his followers' (2:13-17). The ubiquitous scribes have observed this (as well as being in houses, at synagogues and in the cornfields) and complain. Jesus' answer is plainly spoken: 'It is not the healthy who need the doctor, but the sick. I did not come to call the virtuous, but sinners.'

By this stage, Jesus' preaching of the Kingdom and his ministry were taking shape. He continues to heal, often upset by the spying that was now taking place so that the authorities might trap him. When he cures the man with a withered hand on the Sabbath – 'is it against the law on the Sabbath to do good, or to do evil; to save life or to kill?' – he is 'grieved at their obstinacy' and looks angrily round at them. And, with good reason, because it is after this that the Pharisees and the Herodians begin to plot against him, 'discussing how to destroy him' (3:1-6).

Crowds still follow him. He picks his twelve who 'were to be his companions and to be sent out to preach' (3:13-19). But he has trouble with his family. First they want to rescue him because, with such crowds, he could not even have a meal and they were convinced he was out of his mind (3:20-21). Later his mother (the only reference to her in Mark's Gospel) and other relatives seek him and send in a message. He takes the opportunity to say that his mother and brothers are anyone who does the will of God (3:31-35). This may not have changed their minds about his mental condition!

Jesus the Teacher

Throughout the Gospel, sections of teaching can be found. The first of these is a collection of parables (4:1-34). One might say that Mark's Gospel is light on parables. The familiar parable of the Sower (and its explanation) is there along with short parables of the lamp, the measure, the seed growing by itself, the mustard seed. Mark sums up, 'Using many parables like these, he spoke the word to them, so far as they were capable of understanding it. He would not speak to them except in parables, but he explained everything to his disciples when they were alone' (v. 33-34). Later, Jesus refers to the fig tree as a parable for the eschatological times (13:28-32), but he gives only one more parable in the context of his passion and that is the parable of the wicked tenants of the vineyard who killed the owner's son (12:1-10). One has to go to Matthew and Luke for parables.

In Jesus' teaching in Mark, there are also the foundations of discourses that will be amplified, especially by Matthew.

The twelve receive a brief mission instruction (6:7-13). There is a longer warning against the scribes and the Pharisees. Whilst some of these attacks will be considerably developed in Matthew 23, Mark's condemnations have a practicality and down-to-earth tone about them that is missing from the other Gospels. The discourse in 7:1-23 is one of the longest consistent passages in Mark. Jesus outlines ritual regulations observed by the religious leaders, about washing hands and about washing 'arms as far as the elbow' (v. 3), about sprinklings and about the washing of cups, pots and bronze dishes (v. 4). These retorts to criticisms that the disciples ate with unclean hands lead to a fulfilment text, a direct quote from the Jewish Scriptures that is seen as being fulfilled. It is from Isaiah 29:3 about people honouring God with their lips 'while their hearts are far from me' (v. 6-7). Jesus even quotes the decalogue, the commandment on honouring father and mother, and denounces the ways that the religious leaders get round the commandment by offering to God their personal money that they could have used to help their parents. 'In this way you make God's will null and void for the sake of your tradition' (v. 8-13). He takes up the theme briefly again in 12:38-40.

Jesus gets even earthier when talking about goodness and evil, indicating that whatever is eaten goes into the stomach and out into the sewer and is not unclean. It is the evil in the heart that comes out of the heart into action that makes people unclean (v. 14-23).

Other brief discourses can be found on discipleship, 'What does it profit to lose one's soul...? Take up your cross...' (8:34-91); on scandal and millstones around necks (9:42-50); on divorce (10:1-12); on the danger of riches, after the encounter with the rich young man (10:17-31); on leadership and true authority, after James and John (instead of their mother as in Matthew) ask for thrones at Jesus' right and left in the kingdom (10:41-5); and an eschatological discourse which is directly followed by Mark's passion narrative (13:1 37).

Jesus also engages, using wit and shrewdness, with scribes and Pharisees about the significance of John's baptism (11:27-33). He argues about coins belonging to God or Caesar and, while this is very familiar and often quoted, Mark notes that 'this reply took them completely by surprise' (12:13-17). And there is the confrontation about the resurrection of the dead with the Sadducees who did not believe in it and who over-dramatise a scenario about seven brothers marrying the one woman and turn it into a riddle, asking whose wife she would be in heaven (12:18-27). But there is a more positive interchange about the greatest commandment of all (12:28-34).

Jesus in Action

Mark's Gospel prefers to offer the actions of Jesus, many of them miracles. And they often contain lively detail.

Commentators note that in the story of the calming of the storm (4:35-41), it is the Gospel of Mark that says that Jesus 'was in the stern, his head on the cushion, asleep'. It is Mark who states vividly, 'and the wind dropped'.

In Mark, the first miracle of the loaves (6:30-44) is preceded by the remark that Jesus felt sorry for the crowds because they were like sheep without a shepherd and he set himself to teach them at some length. With this introduction of the shepherd theme, writers have speculated that this account of the loaves is presented in the framework of Psalm 23, that God is the shepherd and so is Jesus. He gives people rest – in fact, the people are asked to sit down in groups, out there in the lonely place although there were farms and villages about, on 'the green grass in squares of hundreds and fifties' where they are fed abundantly. Later, when it is dark and the apostles are in valleys of darkness made by the waves with the wind against them, they glimpse Jesus, thinking at first he is a ghost walking on the water, but then he reassures them and they are comforted. The wind drops again.

In the second miracle of the loaves (8:1-10), the people have been with Jesus for three days in a deserted place and there is nowhere to buy food. He is concerned that 'if I send them home hungry, they will collapse on the way'. The two fish have been in each of these narratives. One narrative refers to five loaves, the other to seven. The baskets of scraps are twelve and then seven. Jesus' giving of food is abundant.

What is significant about the witness of the Markan community is that in so many of the narratives (as has already been noted with the healing of the paralytic, the calming of the storm and the miracles of the loaves), there is much more detail in the Markan accounts, despite Mark's being the shortest Gospel of the four, than in the accounts of the same events in the other Synoptics.

The classic passage that was often included in the old seminary textbooks for the *Introduction to the New Testament* course was 5:21-43, two miracles, one the healing of the woman with the haemorrhage, the other the raising of the daughter of Jairus from the dead. When the passages from Matthew and Luke were printed beside that of Mark, the Markan account took up far more space than the other two. The difference is in the detail.

Matthew (9:18-26) introduces the events plainly. Jesus is talking to the crowds. Luke (8:40-56) has Jesus returning from a trip and being welcomed by the large crowd, personalising the plainness of Matthew's style. Mark amplifies. Jesus has 'crossed again in the boat to the other side'. A large crowed had gathered round him 'and he stayed by the lakeside'.

For Matthew, an official, unnamed, comes to Jesus, bows low in reverence and puts his request: his daughter has just died; will Jesus come and lay his hand on her and 'her life will be saved'. Without demur, Jesus and the disciples rise and follow him.

Luke's account at this moment is quite vivid. The official is from the synagogue. He has a name, Jairus. He falls at Jesus' feet, pleading that Jesus come to the house. His daughter (and Luke, not Mark this time, adds that she is twelve years old) is not dead but dying. Luke adds further that 'the crowds were almost stifling Jesus as he went'.

Mark's version is similar. The man's name is Jairus. He is an official. He falls at Jesus' feet. His 'little daughter is desperately sick'. His request is for Jesus to come and lay his hands on her 'and make her better and save her life'. Jesus goes with Jairus, a large crowd pressing round him.

At this point in each Gospel, the narrative moves to the story of the woman with the haemorrhage.

Matthew's account is brief and succinct. The essential elements are there: the illness for twelve years, her touching the fringe of Jesus' cloak; Jesus turning and seeing her and offering her courage, stating that her faith has restored her to health; the woman is instantly cured.

Luke mentions the twelve years and adds that no one was able to cure her. But Mark's version exemplifies the fuller treatment his Gospel gives: 'after long and painful treatment under various doctors, she had spent all she had without being any the better for it, in fact, she was getting worse.' It is hard to know whether the Markan community knew the actual details of the woman or whether they were just good storytellers.

The narrative continues with the information that she had heard about Jesus and had determined that if she could touch even his clothes, she would be well again. Mark and Luke mention that she came up behind him, putting him in the predicament that he knew someone had touched him but did not know who or why. In Matthew, Jesus simply turns round and speaks to the woman. Luke says Jesus asks who touched him. Mark says Jesus asks who touched his clothes. It is Peter, specifically in Luke, and the disciples who tell Jesus it is the crowd pushing. Mark has the disciples putting a touch more exasperation into their reply, 'You see how the crowd is pressing round you and yet you say, "Who touched my clothes?"' That did not satisfy Jesus. 'He continued to look all around to see who had done it.'

As regards the healing itself, Luke says that the haemorrhage stopped at that instant. Mark expands again, 'The source of the bleeding dried up instantly, and she felt in herself that she was cured of the complaint.'

But, the significant experience for Jesus is that Jesus is 'instantly aware' that power had gone out of him. Luke has Jesus say, 'Somebody touched me. I felt that power had gone out from me.'

Both Gospels then have the woman coming forward, trembling. Mark adds 'because she knew what had happened to her'. She falls at Jesus' feet and tells him the whole truth. Jesus bids her go, commending her faith and wishing her peace.

At this stage, the narrative of Jairus' daughter continues. Once again, Matthew has the most direct rendition. After all, unlike the other Gospels, he has the little girl already dead rather than dying. There is commotion. There are flute players. Jesus says, rather abruptly, 'Get out of here; the little girl is not dead, she is asleep.' When they had been 'turned out', Jesus takes her by the hand and she stands up. The news spreads everywhere.

The versions in Mark and Luke are very close indeed. While Jesus is still speaking to the woman with the haemorrhage, messengers come to say that the girl is now dead and that Jesus need not be put to any further trouble.

He overhears this and tells them not to be afraid but to have faith. He then takes Peter, James and John (the three who were witnesses to his transfiguration and to his agony in the garden) with him. They go into the house with the parents of the child. Once again the 'commotion' is noted, a bit more emphasis offered in Mark. The mourners not only wail. They weep and wail unrestrainedly. They laugh at Jesus before they are turned out.

It is in the narrative of the raising that Mark gives more detail. Mark says that Jesus takes his three companions and the child's mother and father into the house. He takes her by the hand and speaks the Aramaic words, '*Talitha, kum*'. The little girl gets up at once. It is now that Mark mentions her age. 'She began to walk about for she was twelve years old.' There is the nice touch in Mark and Luke where Jesus suggests that they give her something to eat. Once again he orders the astonished parents to keep this experience to themselves.

Mark's passion narrative includes an anointing at Bethany by a nameless woman at the house of Simon the Leper. This reminds us of how the stories were told in different ways in the different communities. In John, it is Martha's sister, Mary, who anoints Jesus but at her own home in Bethany with Lazarus, raised from the dead, the honoured guest (although there is a reference to the same Mary having anointed Jesus earlier). In Luke, it is a woman who is a sinner in the city who anoints Jesus. And it is in the house of Simon the Pharisee.

The narrative itself is brief and direct, a succession of events with which we have become familiar, although it is only in Mark where Jesus, in Gethsemane, prays to his father using the more intimate term, 'Abba' (14:36).

Some of the other detail seems to refer to persons known to the Markan community, such as the detail of the young man who had followed Jesus to the garden but who, when the guards caught hold of him, ran away leaving a linen cloth in their hands. It was all he had been wearing (14:51-52). On the way to Calvary the soldiers enlist the help of the passer-by, Simon of Cyrene, who was coming in from the country, to carry Jesus' cross. He is explicitly referred to as the father of Alexander and Rufus (15:21-22). There were women named as watching the crucifixion from a distance, women who had followed Jesus and looked after him when he was in Galilee. The Gospel adds that there were many other women who had come up to Jerusalem with him (15:40-50). This early passion narrative appeals to the witness of those known in the communities to vouch for the truth of the events.

In Mark it is Joseph of Arimathaea, a prominent member of the council, who buries Jesus. The women, including Mary Magdelene, note the site of the grave and then bring spices to anoint the body (15:42-47).

The resurrection narrative (16:1-8) is very brief, ending tentatively with the women going to the tomb wondering how to roll back the large stone at its entrance only to find the tomb empty with a young man announcing that Jesus is risen and that they are to tell the disciples, and Peter, to go to Galilee where they will see him. The women run from the tomb, frightened and do not tell anyone... Here the original Gospel ends.

For completion's sake, at least in comparison with Matthew, Luke and John, a compendium of stories from their Gospels is added.

The Gospel of Mark offers the basic narrative outline of Jesus and his ministry. It is the good news of Jesus from his baptism to his passion, death and resurrection. It is also vivid Good News, Sensate Good News, appealing to the reader to appreciate Jesus in the detail of the successive stories that show how Jesus of Nazareth became the Son of God.

Matthew's Gospel

In Church tradition and in the popular listing of Matthew, Mark, Luke and John, Matthew's Gospel has been considered the first and oldest Gospel. Recent research indicates that, in fact, Mark's is the first Gospel. However, in the second century, about 150 AD, Justin Martyr refers to Matthew's Gospel and a collection of 'sayings', or 'logia', of Jesus. Perhaps the early core of this Gospel consisted of these sayings and that led to Matthew's Gospel being considered the first.

Whatever the date of the compilation of the Gospel, the reference to the 'logia' suggests a way into looking at the style, language and treatment of themes in Matthew's Gospel.

The argument of this chapter is that Matthew's Gospel has a pervading Thinking Function tone. Obviously, as with each Gospel, contributors to the oral tradition and the final written tradition comprised all Types. However, there seems to be a long tradition of seeing Matthew's as the Gospel which put forth clear teaching in a range of discourses and recounted key miracles and parables in orderly category sections of the Gospel.

It is appropriate to consider Matthew's Gospel and Type in a Thinking style and present the points in as clear and structured a way as possible.

The Jewish Background

Matthew's Gospel has more direct quotations from the Jewish Scriptures than the other three Gospels. It also includes more direct references to books and characters from the Jewish Scriptures. The emphasis here is on direct references. The other Gospels certainly contain quotations and references but, often, they use more indirect allusions.

It is said that the community which produced this Gospel was basically Jewish, Jewish converts for whom the interconnection between the Jewish Scriptures and the message of Jesus needed to be developed and spelt out.

Fulfilment Texts

This is immediately evident in the first two chapters of the Gospel, the Infancy Narratives. Chapter one begins with a genealogy to establish Jesus as an authentic Son of David, son of Joseph of the House of David. The three segments of fourteen generations in Jesus' lineage (from Abraham to David, from David to the Babylonian exile, from the Exile to Jesus) is not a literal genealogical tree. Meaning is important. It is pointed out that the Hebrew letters in the name of David, when read and considered, as they are, as numbers, add up to fourteen. Therefore, Jesus is perfectly – with the fourteen presented three times – the Son of David. With this established in a Jewish tradition, the Gospel structures the narrative it presents as meditative stories ('midrash' is the word used to describe a story developed to enhance and interpret a text) centred on specific quotations. The cumulative effect of these stories and quotations is the demonstration that Jesus is to be seen in the light of the tradition and that he is the fulfilment of the tradition. He is truly a prophet and the fulfilment of messianic prophecy (Is 7:14); he is the new shepherd leader in the line of David (Mic 5:1); he is to be seen as the new Moses, miraculously saved as an infant and with a connection to Egypt (Hos 11:1); a prophetic sign of contradiction and grief (Jer 31:15); and a Galilean from Nazareth (the quotation used cannot be found as such in the Jewish Scriptures).

The parallels with Moses are significant. Matthew's Gospel presents Jesus in comparison with other biblical figures, like Jonah and Solomon. And the text adds the statement, 'but a greater than (Jonah or Solomon) is here'. Jesus, therefore, in the Infancy Narratives, is greater than Moses. Jesus will give statements of new law on a mountain (the Sermon on the Mount, ch. 5-7) and Moses will appear at Jesus' transfiguration (17:1-8).

Jesus' authority and leadership are also strong themes in these chapters. Magi from the east, with symbolic gifts of gold, frankincense and myrrh, go to Herod the king for information about the fulfilment of prophecy. They travel to Bethlehem to find the child. Regal personages pay homage to Jesus.

The presentation of Mary in Matthew's Gospel is not personalised as in Luke's Infancy Narratives. The emphasis is on Joseph and his relationship to Mary, the law of betrothal and divorce, the divine conception of Jesus and his birth, and God revealing action steps to Joseph in dreams (echoing the patriarch from the book of Genesis, Joseph, the interpreter of dreams). After Jesus' birth, Mary's presence is always linked with that of Jesus. The phrase used is, 'the child and his mother' (2:11, 13, 14, 20, 21).

Mark and Luke use fulfilment texts for the beginning of Jesus' ministry, especially Isaiah 40:3 highlighting the highway through the desert for the new exodus. So also does Matthew. Luke, like Matthew, uses text debates between Jesus and the Satan for the temptation of Jesus in the desert (ch. 4). The same texts are used. However, Matthew's ending to the narrative is more direct and brusque than that of Luke, 'Be off, Satan' (4:10).

In the main body of the Gospel, almost all the fulfilment texts come from the book of Isaiah: 8:23, 9:1 is used to introduce Jesus' ministry, beginning in Galilee (4:12-17); 53:4 is used to show Jesus' miracles are signs of his suffering to take away people's sins (8:16-17); Malachi 3:1 is introduced to indicate to the Baptist and his disciples who Jesus is (11:2-15); this theme is further developed by reference to the first Servant Song in Isaiah 42:1-4 (12:15-21), that Jesus is to be seen as the Servant; the failure of Jesus' listeners to understand his parables elicits a quotation from Isaiah 6:9-10 (13:10-17) backed up by Psalm 78:3 (13:34-35) and the hypocrisy of the Pharisees is condemned through Isaiah 29:13 (15:1-9).

Another group of fulfilment texts is used in the Passion narrative, especially linked with Jesus' triumphal entry into Jerusalem (ch. 21). The king riding on the donkey (Zech 9:9) is linked with several quotations from the psalms.

Matthew's Gospel also has Jesus use quotations and references to the Jewish Scriptures throughout the Sermon on the Mount in his comparisons with the old law and his teaching, in his debates with both the Pharisees and Sadducees: Genesis 1:27 for teaching on marriage (19:1-9); the prescriptions of the Decalogue from both Exodus and Deuteronomy for the rich young man (19:16-22); witness to testimony (18:15-18), Exodus 3:6 against the Sadducees to prove the resurrection from the dead (22:23-33); the expressions of the greatest commandments of the law from Deuteronomy 6:5 and Leviticus 19:18 (22:34-40).

Apocalyptic Literature

One of the features of the literature of what is called the intertestamental period was its apocalyptic imagery and vocabulary. As early as the 6th century BC, influenced by their exile in Babylon, inspired writers started to use highly imaginative language and metaphors. Dead bones became enfleshed and came alive. Gog of Magog fought battles of light and darkness at Armageddon.

As the centuries passed, this kind of colourful and

hyperbolic literature developed and created an apocalyptic mentality and apocalyptic expectations (not unlike some current millennial outpourings). This can be seen in the book of Daniel. A symbol of this is the expectation of the dramatic return of Elijah who was remembered as not dying but going up to the heavens in a fiery chariot.

While the New Testament book of Revelation is a biblical culmination of this literature, many of the books, including the synoptic Gospels, share this apocalyptic imagination. Matthew's Gospel has two chapters permeated by this apocalyptic perspective (chs. 24-25), chapter 25 containing three parables, the bridesmaids, the talents and the judgement, all of which have apocalyptic conclusions.

Commentators suggest that Matthew's community is concerned with the Roman destruction of Jerusalem and the Temple in 70 AD. With the community seeing itself as Jewish converts, the problem of continuity with the Jewish tradition was disturbed by the rejection of Christianity by Jewish leaders and the Roman invasion. Chapter 24 develops allusions to disasters in Jewish history, to Noah and the flood, to Daniel and the setting up of the statue of Jupiter, the 'disastrous abomination', in the Temple, as well as to the arising of false prophets trying to deceive the faithful. It is, in the language of the prophets, the 'Day of the Lord' – but it has become more cosmically vast.

It culminates, as do the Jewish Scriptures, with the vision of the coming of the Son of Man on the clouds of heaven to receive the inheritance of the promises made to Abraham (Daniel 7). Jesus is presented as the fulfilment of the apocalypse. He is the Son of Man, a claim also put forward during his passion, to the chief priests and the Sanhedrin (26:57-68).

Fulfilment texts inviting readers to understand the truth of the claims of Jesus in the light of the Jewish Scriptures are a prominent feature of Matthew's Gospel and an invitation to use the Thinking Function to understand who Jesus is.

Structure of the Gospel

Matthew's Gospel has a more orderly structure than the other three Gospels which have their own particular perspectives on the Good News. It begins, as has been seen, with the genealogy of Jesus, laying the claim for him to be the true Son of David. It finishes with Jesus having completed his prophetic mission of preaching God's Kingdom, of his having suffered in the pattern of the prophets and of his being the true Servant of Yahweh (Is chs. 42-53) who is raised in glory after suffering for the salvation of all people. This gives Jesus the authority of God. He transmits this to his particularly chosen group of apostles who are to continue his mission. It is presented in Jesus' farewell speech in a threefold manner: the apostles are to preach and make disciples of peoples of all nations; they are to ritualise this discipleship in baptism in the way that we now name 'sacramental', so that they become the people of the new covenant; they are to give Jesus' new law (which is that of loving others as Jesus loved) which is the way of life to be observed by the new covenant people (28:16-20).

The Jerusalem Bible has useful headings to highlight the careful logical structure of the Gospel.

After the Infancy Narratives, 'The Kingdom of Heaven is preached'(chs. 4-7). This includes a narrative section with the beginning of Jesus' ministry (ch. 4) followed by a discourse section, the Sermon on the Mount (chs. 5-7).

There follows a new section where 'The Kingdom is preached' (chs. 8-10). It includes a narrative section which is a collection of miracle stories, ten of them (chs. 8-9) and a discourse section, this time a discourse on discipleship and mission (ch. 9).

As the Gospel progresses, the understanding of the Kingdom deepens, 'The Mystery of the Kingdom of Heaven' (chs. 11-13). Yet again there is a narrative section (chs. 11-12) which includes stories of Jesus' preaching and his acceptance and rejection, some miracles and discussions about good and evil spirits. There is also a discourse section, this time a collection of parables of the kingdom (ch. 13:1-52).

The Gospel now makes a transition from the language of Kingdom to that of Church, 'The Church, First-fruits of the Kingdom of Heaven' (ch. 13:52, ch. 18). The pattern of narrative and discourse continues. The narrative (ch. 13:52, ch. 17) ranges rather widely with key passages including the death of the Baptist, the miracles of the loaves, the promise to Peter (and other Peter-centred stories), the transfiguration and some healings. The next discourse (ch. 18) is considered as a discourse on the Church. However, this section might seem to be a more arbitrary structuring of the Gospel than other divisions.

'The Approaching Advent of the Kingdom of Heaven' (chs. 19-25) is the final section before the Passion and Resurrection. The narrative section (chs. 19-23) has a great deal of variety including quite a number of parables and the diatribe against the hypocrisy of the scribes and Pharisees (ch. 23). The discourse is often referred to as 'The Eschatological Discourse' where the preaching and the parables take on an apocalyptic tone (chs. 24-25).

The Gospel concludes, as do the other Gospels, with its Passion and Resurrection narrative (chs. 27-28).

While one can trace the story of Jesus' ministry, the juxtaposition of narrative and discourse emphasises the Gospel's 'logia', the sayings of Jesus referred to at the beginning of this chapter. They give Matthew's Gospel its particular style and its particular communication of the Good News.

With the gathering together of an initial group of miracles (chs. 8-9) and an initial group of parables (ch. 13:1-52) and the Sermon on the Mount (chs. 5-7), the Matthaean community shows itself to be a carefully thinking community which appreciates the truth of Jesus' preaching.

This is confirmed by the comments that the people make at the end of the Sermon on the Mount, 'his teaching made a deep impression on them, because he taught with authority, not as their own scribes' (7:28-29). This authority seems to consist of strong convictions, clearly stated and logically and religiously justified.

The Law

Law is important in Matthew's Gospel. The Sermon on the Mount is new law, given by the new Moses. However, Jesus is at pains to highlight the continuity between the old law and the new. Early in the sermon Jesus says:

> Do not imagine that I have come to abolish the Law or the Prophets. I have come not to abolish but to complete them. I tell you solemnly, till heaven and earth disappear, not one dot, not one little stroke, shall disappear from the Law, until its purpose is achieved.
>
> Therefore, whoever infringes even one of the least of these commandments and teaches others to do the same will be considered least in the kingdom of heaven; but whoever keeps them and teaches them will be considered great in the kingdom of heaven (5:17-19).

Jesus keeps the letter of the law in urging the cured leper to present himself to the priest to verify his healing and to offer the prescribed sacrifice (8:4); he pays the tax for himself and Peter (17:24-27); he interprets divorce law strictly (19:1-9).

However, a challenge to the Thinking Function is the

broad interpretation of law, acting on its spirit. The episode of the walk through the corn fields on the Sabbath and the disciples picking ears of corn – was it lawful for Jesus, for the disciples and for the Pharisees who were there to notice what went on, to be walking in the fields? – gives Jesus the opportunity to explain that necessity might require a literal breaking of the law. He gives the example of the hungry David and his followers eating the loaves reserved for the priests as well as the example of the priests literally breaking the law as they performed their temple duties. Jesus makes the claim to be Master of the Sabbath for, 'a greater than the Temple is here'. And for the more personalised motivation for these interpretations of law, he quotes Hosea 6:6 which says that God is more delighted with compassion than with the formal offering of sacrifice.

This more tempered understanding of law and authority is very clear in 20:20-28. The mother of James and John requested the impossible of Jesus, wanting places of honour in the kingdom. Later the other ten, indignant with the brothers, argued about their own positions. The Master of the Sabbath encapsulated his approach to honour, authority and service, decrying authoritarianism as 'pagan':

> You know that among the pagans the rulers lord it over them and their great men make their authority felt. This is not to happen among you. No; anyone who wants to be great among you must be your servant, and anyone who wants to be first among you must be your slave, just as the Son of Man came not to be served but to serve, and to give his life as a ransom for many.

'No Frills' Language

Although it depends on the quality of the translation of the Gospel, one can hear a particular tone of voice and modulation in each of the Gospels, an indication of how it should be proclaimed in liturgy. It might be said that Matthew's Gospel, while polished, is unvarnished. It is 'no frills' language, plain and to the point. For instance, the introduction to the chapter on parables (ch. 13) gives a setting in the most direct way, 'That same day Jesus left the house and sat by the lakeside, but such crowds gathered round him that he got into a boat and sat there. The people all stood on the beach, and he told them many things in parables.

He said... And the parable of the sower begins at once, 'Imagine a sower going out to sow...'

The chapter continues in that vein, 'He put another parable before them...' (v. 24,31). 'He told them another parable...' (v. 33). 'In all this Jesus spoke to the crowds in parables; indeed he would never speak to them except in parables' (v. 34) and there follows a fulfilment text. Several of the parables that have stayed in the Church's memory and have become part of the metaphorical language of the culture consist of merely two lines: the treasure in the field and, especially, the pearl of great price (v. 44-46).

While Jesus explains the parables to the disciples in the plainest way, making explicit the allegorical parallels in the parable of the sower (v. 18-23) and the weeds (v. 36-43), Matthew's parables of the kingdom chapter ends, '"Have you understood all this?" They said, "Yes".' No extraneous material! 'Well then, every scribe who becomes a disciple of the kingdom of heaven is like a householder who brings out from his storeroom things both new and old' (v. 51-52).

The Sermon on the Mount is one of the best examples of direct language. If the Thinking Function emphasises objectivity, principles, logic and consequences in decision-making, then the principles of the Sermon on the Mount, which have guided Christians and have impressed non-

Christians, are exemplary Thinking Function statements of moral values; for instance:

> Do not judge and you will not be judged; because the judgements you give are the judgements you will get, and the amount you measure out is the amount you will be given. Why do you observe the splinter in your brother's eye and never notice the plank in your own? How dare you say to your brother, 'Let me take the splinter out of your eye', when all the time there is a plank in your own? Hypocrite! Take the plank out of your own eye first, and then you will see clearly enough to take the splinter out of your brother's eye (7:1-5).

The Jerusalem Bible heading for most of the material in chapter 6 is, 'The new standards higher than the old'. Jesus is presented as the teacher par excellence. He speaks clearly and with authority and conviction. He quotes the tradition of the Jewish Scriptures and uses direct quotations. He sets up and elaborates on the previous standards ('of old it was said to you... eye for an eye, tooth for a tooth') then, in his own name ('but I say to you...'), sets the standards higher: 'love your enemies, do good to those who persecute you...'.

The principles of the Sermon almost serve as a charter or guidelines for a Constitution for Christianity.

This direct approach is probably summed up in the well-known dictum from this section of the Sermon.

> All you need to say is 'Yes' if you mean yes, and 'No' if you mean no; anything more than this comes from the evil one (5:37).

Challenge before Harmony

The Thinking Function prizes justice and truth. Harmony and well-being derive from them and not vice versa. The

Thinker does not usually find it difficult to point out errors and to issue challenges. This, as has been seen, is one of the great strengths of the Sermon on the Mount and of the other discourses.

But Matthew's Gospel dramatises Jesus as a challenger. Soon after Peter's profession of faith and the promise of the keys of the kingdom, Peter remonstrates with Jesus, stating that Jesus should not suffer and die. Jesus rounds on him instantly, 'Get behind me Satan! You are an obstacle in my path, because the way you think is not God's way but the human way' (16:21-23).

However, it is the religious leaders, the chief priests, the scribes and the Pharisees, who bear the brunt of Jesus' vigorous and profound challenges. Soon after Jesus' direct action in the expulsion of the dealers from the temple, they want to know on what authority he acts in the way that he does. Jesus uses debating tactics in reply, asking them to justify their response to John the Baptist's preaching. He traps them in a dilemma. If John is from God, they can be challenged for not believing in him. If John's mission is merely human, then the people will react against them since they believe he was from God. They refuse to respond. Jesus, therefore, does not have to tell them on what authority he preaches.

The 'render to Caesar the things that are Caesar's' is an even better known example of Jesus using his wit, wits and debating skills.

But the principal chapter where Jesus challenges, no holds barred, is chapter 23. For 37 verses (and Luke's parallel in 11:37-54 seems a touch genteel in comparison), Jesus is in full blast, 'Scribes and Pharisees, you hypocrites…'. It is eloquent invective, grounded in the religious abuses that Jesus condemns:

> Alas for you, scribes and Pharisees, you hypocrites! You who are like whitewashed tombs that look handsome on

the outside, but inside are dead men's bones and every kind of corruption. In the same way you appear to people from the outside like good honest men, but inside you are full of hypocrisy and lawlessness (23:27-28).

Jesus also challenges the authorities during his passion, whether it be his defence in Gethsemane, that he had been teaching in the temple and that they had been too afraid to arrest him, but were taking him like a brigand in the garden (26:47-56), or in his silence when questioned by Pilate (27:14).

Parables of Justice

A particular feature of each Gospel is the collection of parables that appear only in that Gospel and what these parables have in common.

The parables exclusive to Matthew's Gospel are:

1. the parable of the weeds growing with the wheat (13:24-30);
2. the treasure in the field (13:44);
3. the pearl of great price (13:45-46);
4. the dragnet (13:47-50);
5. the unforgiving debtor (18:23-35);
6. the labourers in the vineyard (20:1-16);
7. the two sons working in the vineyard (21:28-31);
8. the ten bridesmaids (25:1-13);
9. the last judgement (25:31-46).

The first four of these parables are parables of the kingdom told in connection with the parable of the sower. The other six concern work in some way and are linked with parables common to other Gospels, specifically the parable of the talents, of the wedding feast and the killing of the son of the owner of the vineyard. Accompanying the images of work are issues of human justice. The parable of the labourers in the vineyard could have ended with the owner paying each of the workers a proportionate wage. Justice would be seen to be served.

However, these parables move their readers on to an understanding of justice beyond mere distributive justice. God is the owner of the vineyard. God pays each worker the agreed upon wage. But God is also able to be lavish, extravagant in giving his wealth to those who may not, by contract, deserve it. This is the point (in reverse, perhaps) of the unforgiving servant demanding the letter of the contract without mercy, whereas God, the king, is lavish.

The passion narrative begins, 'Jesus had now finished all he wanted to say'(26:1) (after all, it is the Gospel of the 'logia', the sayings of Jesus). This means that the last word that Jesus wanted to say was the parable of the eschatological judgement, the justice judgement, where those who combined their love of God with love of neighbour, even when they did not realise it, were fulfilling the whole law. And the kingdom, therefore, was theirs: 'Come, you whom my father has blessed, take for your heritage the kingdom prepared for you since the foundation of the world' (25:34).

Jesus, as in the other Gospels, is the master storyteller. His parables have become classics. In Matthew, the parables are plain, direct, certainly unsentimental (even, sometimes, harsh in tone) and are concerned with justice and the fulfilment of the law.

Jesus and Encounters

There are appreciable differences in the Matthaean narratives of Jesus' encounters from those in other Gospels. Two examples: the Canaanite woman (15:21-28) and the Centurion (8:5-13).

The incident of the Canaanite woman is also found in Mark 7:24-30. There it takes its place as another miracle at a time when Jesus did not want to be recognised. The woman hears about Jesus and comes to him, concerned about her 'little daughter'. She begs Jesus for a cure. They exchange the famous bargaining words about the children being fed and it not being fair to take their food and throw it to the dogs and her quipping that the house-dogs under the table eat the children's scraps. Jesus is impressed and sends her home, reassured, where she finds 'the child lying on the bed and the devil gone'.

Jesus seems far more antagonistic or confronting in the Matthew version. Jesus had withdrawn to the region about Tyre and Sidon. The woman comes out shouting and pleading to the Son of David for her daughter. But Jesus does not answer her at all. It is too much for the disciples, who plead with him to grant her request so that they can be rid of her and her shouting. Jesus begins by justifying his silence, 'I was sent only to the lost sheep of the House of Israel.' The bargaining repartee then follows with the woman, who had now come up to him, kneeling at his feet. Jesus commends her faith and her daughter gets well again.

The theme of the Jews' not recognising Jesus and the Gentiles, the latecomers to God's history of salvation, appears all through Matthew's Gospel. It is often a key punch-line to parables or incidents where many are called and few are chosen. The encounter with the Syro-Phoenician woman is one. So also is the encounter with the centurion, whose words are also well-known.

The contrast between the Lukan and Matthaean versions of this story are quite marked. In Luke it is the Jewish elders whom the centurion sends to plead his cause. The servant is a favourite of the centurion and is sick and near death. The elders enhance their request with the information that the centurion was very friendly towards the people and had built the synagogue. 'He deserves this of you'. It is when Jesus is near the house that the centurion sends word to say that Jesus should not put himself to the trouble of coming because he is not worthy to have Jesus under his roof. He then speaks the words about being under authority himself as well as having people under him. Jesus is astonished and praises his faith, greater than any he has found in Israel. The messengers go back and the servant is in perfect health. The centurion does not meet Jesus.

Matthew's version is more direct and up front. The centurion approaches Jesus and pleads with him. The servant is paralysed and in great pain. Jesus offers to go to cure him but the centurion demurs, not worthy to have Jesus under his roof. He need only say the word and the servant would be healed. He elaborates on being under authority and having servants at his command.

Jesus not only praises the centurion's faith. He takes the opportunity to make one of his fullest statements about the failure of many of the children of Abraham, Isaac and Jacob to come to the final banquet in the kingdom. They will be turned out into the dark and many gentiles will come to take their place. The servant is healed.

There is great emotion in many of Jesus' encounters in Matthew's Gospel. However, they are recounted with great objectivity rather than highlighting good feelings and harmony.

Women in Matthew's Gospel

When considered alongside the other Gospels, Matthew's Gospel introduces comparatively few women. One wonders how this reflects the role and status of women in the Matthaean community and the Jewish tradition of the place of women in society. Listing the women, we find, after Mary the mother of Jesus in the Infancy Narratives, Peter's mother-in-law healed in 8:14-15 where she immediately gets up to wait on Jesus; the woman with the haemorrhage and the daughter of Jairus both healed with tender words and gestures in 9:18-26; his mother and relations, 'anxious to have a word with him' in 12:46-50; the woman in the parable of the yeast, 13:33; Herodias and her daughter asking for John the Baptist's head, 14:3-12; the Syro-Phoenician woman, 15:21-28; the mother of James and John trying to book thrones at Jesus' right hand in his kingdom for her sons, 20:20-23; a brief warning in the eschatological times, 'Alas for those who are with child, or with babies at the breast', 24:19; the ten bridesmaids of the parable, 25:1-13; the woman who anoints Jesus at Bethany and whom he defends, 26:6-13; Mary of Magdala and the other women watching at Calvary and who sat vigil at the sepulchre and then went to visit, 27:55-56, 61, 28:1-10. As with all the other Gospels, it is Mary Magdalene who is the first witness to the Risen Lord and who is commissioned to let the brothers know and to tell them where to meet him.

Some of the women are significant, especially their presence at Jesus' death and as witnesses to his resurrection, but this is a small presence compared with that in the other Gospels. All the verses of Matthew's Gospel which present women would scarcely add up to the verses in John 4 with the story of the woman at the well.

Statistically, it is said that, in western cultures, 70-75% of men identify with the Thinking Function. Matthew's Gospel seems to be a male-oriented Gospel. This means, of course, that it is a challenge to the Feeling Function of both men and women.

Luke's Gospel

The Gospel of compassion has been one of the traditional descriptions for Luke's Gospel. Perhaps the reason for this was that there was a tradition that Luke was a doctor – and that the tradition had a high opinion of sympathetic doctor patient relationships! It was also said that a reason for the humane tone of the Gospel was that one of the major sources for the events recounted was Mary, the mother of Jesus, especially, of course, for the Infancy Narratives. Commentators pointed out that many encounters and parables occur only in this Gospel and that they all illustrate the compassion of Jesus.

It is an easy Type step to move from this traditional understanding of Luke's Gospel to seeing it as a Feeling Function Gospel. It is a Gospel which, while it does not avoid putting Jesus in confrontational situations, avoids confrontation and offers stories of harmony. Highlighting this harmony will be one of the main features of this survey of the Gospel of Luke.

The Lukan community was predominantly gentile rather than Jewish. While there was a familiarity with the Jewish Scriptures, they were not incorporated so readily into the Gospel as fulfilment texts as in Matthew's Gospel or even John's. Rather, the Jewish Scriptures pervade the Gospel of Luke.

Another feature of Luke is the wide range of characters who appear in this Gospel and in no other. In the Infancy Narratives alone there are Zechariah and Elizabeth, angel Gabriel, the shepherds at Bethlehem, Simeon and Anna, the elders in the Temple. In the Gospel proper there are the widow of Naim, the women who accompany Jesus, the crippled woman in the synagogue, the man with dropsy, the ten lepers, Zacchaeus, the women on the way to Calvary, the good thief, the disciples on the road to Emmaus. And some of the classic parables, especially the Prodigal Son, the Good Samaritan, the Pharisee and the Publican, the Rich Man and the Poor Man are to be found only in Luke.

Style and Structure

The Lukan community acknowledged the Graeco-Roman culture of the readers of the Gospel and so used some of the literary conventions of the time. The Introduction (1:1-4) is akin to the formal prefaces used by historians. Readers familiar with Herodatus or Thucydides, Livy or Cato would recognise that this approach was being used in this Gospel, the story of a great man, based on personal testimony (not archival accuracy) which would promote and enhance the reputation of the subject.

Another feature of Luke's writings, Luke-Acts, is that the centre of the work, both structurally and thematically, is Jerusalem. From chapter 9:51 Jesus is presented as making his way steadily towards Jerusalem. Jerusalem is David's city, the city of the Temple, the covenant city where God's promises are to be accomplished. Jesus is welcomed into Jerusalem. The Last Supper takes place there. Jesus' agony in the garden, passion and death take place in Jerusalem. And the resurrection. (The disciples walk to Emmaus away from Jerusalem but, on encountering Jesus, they hurry back to Jerusalem.) Jesus ascends from Jerusalem. The Spirit descends on the disciples in Jerusalem and it is there that the first sermons are preached, the first community of disciples is formed. Then, from Jerusalem, the message, first through Peter and, then, through Paul, is preached in Samaria and, ultimately, to the ends of the earth.

The Graeco-Roman literary style, combined with the Jewish scriptural heritage, means that Jesus is both hero and fulfilment of the covenant promises. The stories and the telling are enhanced by these two perspectives.

Prologue to Ministry: The Infancy Narratives

The Lukan narratives are in strong contrast to the stylised fulfilment texts and midrashic stories of Matthew's Gospel. In Luke we have a number of characters, indeed of personalities. While there are the accounts of the origins of Jesus, we also can discern a 'biography' of Mary from the Annunciation to the beginning of Jesus' ministry.

Contrasting parallels are made between the annunciation of a marvellous conception to Zechariah (he doubts and is struck dumb) and the annunciation of an even more marvellous conception to Mary (she questions in trust and speaks her 'let it be done to me' as she commits herself as the Lord's handmaid). Contrasting parallels are also made between the birth of John the Baptist, supported by Mary's visitation to his mother, her cousin Elizabeth, who is surrounded by family and friends while, at the birth of Jesus in the stable at Bethlehem, Jesus, Mary and Joseph are surrounded by shepherds and animals.

These narratives are full of motifs with allusions to the Jewish Scriptures and contain two psalm-like hymns of God's promises and their fulfilment, spoken by Mary (1:46-55) and Zechariah (1:67-79).

The annunciation to Mary illustrates the wealth of these motifs and allusions. These include: the messenger of God to Mary, Gabriel, the angel of Daniel 8:16, the angel who announces the fullness of time; Mary betrothed to Joseph of the House of David whose descendants would receive the covenant promises and rule with a reign that has no end (2 Sam 7); Gabriel's words of greeting and urging Mary not to be afraid echoing greetings to mothers of saviours like the mother of Gideon (Judg 6:12) and the mother of Samson (Judg 13:1-7); Mary rejoicing like the daughter of Sion because the Lord was in her (Zeph 3:14-18)... The Infancy Narratives are filled with this scriptural poetic richness.

Jesus' birth is situated within the history of the Roman empire of which Judaea was a province. Joseph and Mary fulfil the obligation of the census taken at the time of Caesar Augustus (2:1-5) as well as the traditions of Jewish law, with circumcision (2:21) and with the sacrifices for the presentation and consecration of the child (2:22-28). On this occasion, Simeon the sage and Anna the prophetess greet the child and Simeon offers a psalm-canticle of peace for the fulfilment of God's promises.

The Jewish law and background are to the fore in the narrative of Jesus lost in the Temple and his discussions with the teachers. Luke has recounted how Jesus grew as a human being, 'the child grew to maturity and he was filled with wisdom and God's favour was with him' (2:40). Christians have not been as familiar with Jewish traditions as they might. There is still some surprise when it is suggested that this story (2:41-50) is a Bar Mitzvah story. Jesus was at the age where he was initiated as an adult into his society. He prayed and read the Scriptures in public. Nevertheless, he then returned to Nazareth with Mary and Joseph and 'lived under their authority... And Jesus increased in wisdom, in stature and in favour with God and with all' (2:51-52).

Throughout the whole Gospel, the Lukan community presupposes what theologians call a 'Low Christology', a theology of Jesus which presents him as fully human and then gradually moves through his life and his mission to appreciate the place of the divine in his life. This conclusion to the Infancy Narratives states succinctly how Jesus grew as a human being.

The portrait of Mary is another feature of the Infancy Narratives. She is the young virgin of Nazareth betrothed to Joseph. She experiences, in a quiet way, what the prophets of Israel experienced: a consecration, a special call, the listening to and acceptance of God's word for a mission. Mary, pregnant with God's Word, is likened to the Ark of the Covenant, travelling around Israel. However, those who touched the Ark died. Those who encounter Mary, on the other hand, like her cousin Elizabeth, sense life (John leaping in his mother's womb). Mary is greeted as blessed with salutations echoing those of the heroines Jael (Judg 5:24) and Judith (13:18). Mary herself proclaims God's greatness and her blessing in a hymn which echoes the themes of the blessings of the virtuous from the Psalms, especially those who are barren and who conceive, like Samuel's mother, Hannah, in the first chapter of 1 Samuel.

Mary gives birth in the stable, wraps her child in swaddling clothes and lays him in the manger. She listens to what the shepherds have to say. The narrative then highlights a quality of Mary, 'she treasured all these things and pondered them in her heart' (2:19) and, later, 'she stored up all these things in her heart' (2:51).

Mary has Jesus circumcised and presented according to the Law. But the encounter with Simeon has 'the child's father and mother wondering at the things that were being said about him' (2:33). And Simeon, prophesying that Jesus would be a sign of contradiction, says that Mary will also suffer, a sword piercing her soul.

We find that Mary and Joseph were devout. They went from Nazareth to Jerusalem every year for the Passover. (Jesus seems to have had an exemplary upbringing.) At his Bar Mitzvah age they lose him – it is interesting to see the latitude and trust they give Jesus in his behaviour; they do not even think to look for him until after a day's journey. Mary has to learn, with Jesus' reply about God's business, that her son has to grow up and experience his independence from his parents. Mary stores up all of this in her heart.

Mary's only other appearance in the Gospel is in 8:19-21, where the family comes looking for Jesus. Jesus' answer has sometimes been interpreted as stark and hard, 'My mother and my brothers are those who hear the word of God and put it into practice.' Of course, the Mary who pondered all things in her heart must be, par excellence, the one who heard the word of God and put it into practice.

The only other mention of Mary in the Lukan writings is in the Acts of the Apostles. Mary is among the apostles in continuous prayer in the upper room after Jesus' ascension as they wait for the coming of the Spirit (Acts 1:14).

It can be seen from the outline 'biography' of Mary why tradition considered that she had been the source of the Infancy Narratives. This contrasts with Mary as presented in the other Gospels: Mary's pregnancy and the image of the mother and child in Matthew; Mary at Cana and at the foot of the Cross in John; Mary's virtual absence from Mark.

Jesus' Encounters

Jesus was often judged by the company he kept, especially when he mixed with and ate with tax collectors and prostitutes who were continually seeking him out. Luke's Gospel has Jesus mixing with people in a more personal way than in the other Gospels. One of the best-known episodes is the visit to the home of Martha and Mary (10:38-42). It seems Jesus is comfortable with both sisters after being welcomed by Martha. When Mary sits at Jesus' feet, he allows her to do this even though it is not the custom for women to sit at a teacher's feet as a disciple. When Martha 'who was distracted by all the serving' complains about Mary's not helping, Jesus is able to chide her, especially about her 'worrying and fretting'. Perhaps it was not part of

Graeco-Roman historical style but many latter-day Marthas would like to know how Jesus and the disciples pitched in to clear away and even wash and dry up!

Jesus is also at home at Zacchaeus' house after inviting the little man to come down from his observation tree and inviting himself to dinner (19:1-10). By way of contrast (7:36-50), Jesus accepts an invitation to the home of Simon the Pharisee. It is only when the woman 'who was a sinner in the city' intrudes and anoints Jesus to his host's dismay that Jesus makes the point that Simon had not offered him the ritual and common courtesies of washing and anointing for guests.

The one place he does not seem to be at home in is Nazareth, his own hometown (4:16-30). Initially, he is invited to read from the scroll of Isaiah in the synagogue. The people's response is described in quite Feeling Function words, 'he won the approval of all and they were astonished by the gracious words that came from his lips' (v. 22). However, as soon as he applies the Isaiahan text to himself and his ministry, Jesus the prophet discovers that he is not welcome in his own country. Jesus moves into Thinking mode in his challenge to them, quoting the prophets Elijah and Elisha who worked miracles for foreigners rather than for their own. This is quite a heated confrontation because the citizens of Nazareth are enraged. 'They sprang to their feet and hustled him out of the town' (v. 28-9). Jesus has elicited a violent reaction and they want to throw him from the brow of the hill. But he walks away.

The other situations where Jesus encounters people are the miracles. Again, there is a Feeling tone about them. Probably one of the best-known and loved in Luke is the raising of the dead man at Nain (7:11-17), 'the only son of his mother, and she was a widow'. A large number of the townspeople are there. How is Jesus described? 'When the Lord saw her he felt sorry for her.' He asks her not to cry and touches the bier, speaks to the young man and 'gave him to his mother'.

There is also a pathos in the healing of the ten lepers (17:11-9) who went away rejoicing but only one turning back, 'praising God at the top of his voice, who threw himself at Jesus' feet and thanked him. The man was a Samaritan.' And Jesus allows himself the feelings of disappointment that only one had come back, a foreigner.

The Lukan Feeling tone can be seen when the same event is considered in the more Thinking Gospel of Matthew. This has already been found in the comparison of the versions of the healing of the centurion's servant. It is also evident in the healing of the woman with the haemorrhage, also previously considered (8:43-8 and the three verses in Mt 9:20-22).

In Matthew, there is a plain description of the event. The woman, who had been ill for twelve years and thought that if she touched the edge of his garments, she would be cured, came behind Jesus and touched the fringe of his cloak. Jesus turns, sees her, offers her 'Courage' and affirms her faith. She is well again.

The description of the miracle is basically the same. However, it is the aftermath which is important in Luke. Jesus is very conscious of being touched and asks who it was. Peter and the disciples tell him that it is the crowd around him pushing. But Jesus insists, 'I felt that power had gone out of me.' The woman trembles as she is conscious of being found out and, in front of all the people, she falls at Jesus' feet and explains everything, the touch and the healing. Jesus affirms her faith. And his wish for her is not courage, but peace.

We have a greater feel for both the woman and for Jesus who also seems to be discovering more about his own power, how, with healing, power goes out of him. Mark's version, as we have seen, is longer than that of Luke although it too is concerned with power going out of Jesus, but it amplifies the narrative with more detail and information.

This Feeling tone is found also in Jesus' parables.

Jesus' Parables

Jesus is not presented in the Gospels as someone laughing all the time – or even much of the time. The number of books written about the humour of Jesus is not large.

However, there are some sections of Luke which might be better read with a smile. Jesus has been teaching his disciples to pray, just as John's disciples prayed. He then goes on to tell a story, asking his audience to imagine how they might react when in the middle of the night they go to a friend to borrow some bread for another friend on his travels and they have nothing to offer. Jesus dramatises the man and his children in bed, the door bolted, refusing to get up. And what is Jesus' advice? If friendship won't serve as a motivation, persistence will. Jesus seems to be offering a spirituality of persistence, of pestering until you get what you want (11:5-13).

It is the same with God. Search, knock and the door will be opened. Perhaps Jesus seems to be on a roll. He does a turn, a bit like a stand-up comic. He puts it to his audience: 'What man among you would hand his son a stone when he asked for bread? or hand him a snake instead of a fish? or hand him a scorpion if he asked for an egg?' There might have been some fathers with exasperating children who might have been tempted to call back, 'I would, Jesus'. But Jesus gives the punch-line for his spirituality of persistence, 'If you then, who are evil, know how to give your children what is good… how much more will the heavenly Father give the Holy Spirit to those who ask him?'

The spirituality of persistence makes another appearance in 18:1-8. This time it is in a parable, the clash between the unjust judge and the widow who is aptly described in a word we rarely use, 'importunate'. The judge was a hard-headed type, no respecter of persons, no fearer of God. But the widow who kept on coming to him and saying, 'I want justice from you against my enemy' wore him down. He had refused for a long time. But he finally acknowledged that, although he was no respecter of persons and had no fear of God, he must give her her just rights 'or she will persist in coming and worry me to death.'

Jesus seems to enjoy telling this parable. He adds, 'You notice what the unjust judge has to say?' Then the same kind of punch-line as before, 'Now will not God see justice done to his chosen who cry to him day and night even when he delays to help them?' This is a very practical spirituality.

This last parable is introduced with a prologue sentence: 'Then Jesus told them a parable about the need to pray continually and never lose heart.' This is a characteristic of Luke's Gospel. Key parables are introduced with Jesus' perception of why he is telling the parable.

The parable of the Pharisee and the Publican follows immediately (18:9-14). Its introduction is: 'Jesus spoke the following parable to some people who prided themselves on being virtuous and despised everyone else.'

The parable of the Good Samaritan has an even more elaborate setting. One of the lawyers wanted to disconcert Jesus and questioned him about eternal life. Jesus, the good teacher, answered the question with a question about what the Law itself says, eliciting from the lawyer that he knew the answer and could name love of God and love of neighbour. Jesus applauds his answer and urges him to put it into action.

Like a schoolboy who hasn't got his way in attempting to disconcert the teacher, the lawyer was anxious to justify himself and asked the immortal question, 'And who is my neighbour?'

The parable is one of the most repeated. It has the touch of drama and violence with the man robbed and assaulted. The representatives of God and the Law refuse to touch the man for fear of ritual impurity which would require prayers and ceremonies to make them ready to offer prayer to God. (The old joke is that they passed by on the other side of the road because the man was already robbed!) Jesus knew how to include some potentially offensive material into his Lukan storytelling about unjust judges and proud Pharisees, so here the hero is a loathed foreigner, a Samaritan. The Samaritan's reaction to what he sees contrasts with the religious checking out of rituals and obligations of the priest and the Levite. Instead, as in so many encounters, like that with the leper who pleaded for a cure, Jesus is moved with compassion. As we shall see with the father of the prodigal son, who is also moved with compassion, this is the response of God.

The Samaritan is also like God in binding up the wounds of the injured man. In the prophet Hosea (6:2) and in Isaiah (1:5-6), God is a healer and binder of wounds. And the Samaritan is prudent. He does not try to do more than he can. He lifts the man onto his mount, takes him to the inn and offers financial aid. But he still goes to do whatever he was on his way to, promising to reimburse the innkeeper on his way back. He is not a do-gooder or a self-appointed saviour who feels that he is obliged to take on everything to assist the injured man. He can delegate.

The lawyer seems to acknowledge reluctantly that the Samaritan is the true neighbour. Instead of saying 'correct', as if the lawyer had got an exam question right, Jesus is more demanding. He says, 'Go and do the same yourself.'

It is interesting to note that the passage immediately following the Good Samaritan is one that we have already considered, the visit to Martha and Mary (1:38-42). The two stories need to be read together to understand the dialectic of Jesus' teaching. While he urges love of neighbour, it is not any self-proclaimed doing good. Like Mary, it is first necessary to sit at the Lord's feet and hear and discern what God is asking. Then we can go into action like the Samaritan, giving all our love in the area that God asks of us. Otherwise we are like Martha, worrying and fretting about too many things.

To take this insight further, we find that after the Martha and Mary story is the Lukan version of the Lord's Prayer (11:1-4). Jesus himself prays, discerns God's will before acting. The prayer, with its petitions for honouring God and its petitions for blessings on oneself and neighbours, is the perfect resolution of the paradox of contemplation and action.

But the most popular and most skilful parable in Jesus' repertoire is the parable of the Prodigal Son (15:1-32). Again, it is introduced with a setting that highlights the meaning of the parable. The tax collectors and prostitutes are seeking Jesus' company and he and the disciples are eating with them. As usual, the Pharisees and the scribes complain. Luke then says, 'So'- and it is a 'so', a 'therefore', full of consequences for appreciating Jesus himself and his feelings and vulnerability in his ministry – 'Jesus spoke this parable to them.'

But the main feature is supported by the parable of the lost sheep for men and the lost coin for women, so to speak; the lost son for all listeners. A feminist commentator noted that preachers have no difficulty in speaking about God as a shepherd or as a father, but they rarely speak about God as the woman of the parable. Luke offers God in the image of a woman.

In telling the story of the two sons and their father, Jesus appeals to all parents, the laws of inheritance and the basic dilemma of when to say yes and no to requests. A common phrase is 'playing God' which refers to someone exercising complete control over a situation. When we read Jesus' account of what God is like in this parable, we realise that the use of the phrase 'playing God' is almost blasphemous in this sense. According to Jesus, the only one who does not play God is God. God, drawn here as father, is a most permissive parent. The father allows the son to make his mistakes but keeps the lines of communications open for the time of crisis.

The crisis comes.

Jesus once again includes some material which might be considered offensive to his listeners. When the son has squandered his money and the famine comes, not only can he not eat the unclean meat of the pigs he was tending, the pork, he is not even allowed to eat what the pigs ate, their slop.

When the lost son comes to his senses and returns to his father, Jesus is able to reveal to us in story and in ordinary words and phrases, what God is really like. The father never gives up hope. All the time he is on the lookout for the return. When the boy is a long way off, his father sees him and is moved with compassion. This is the compassion of God.

The father does not calculate how long it will be before the son gets to the gate or the door. Rather, the father takes the initiative and runs to meet him. And when he gets to his son, he does not hold back, waiting for an apology from the wayward man. Without hesitation he clasps him in his arms and kisses him tenderly. According to the Jesus of Luke, God is a loving, embracing and kissing father. He also allows his boy to make the speech of repentance he has rehearsed. The father is sensitive enough to know that humans need to express their sorrow. But, then, his responses are lavish – the best robe, ring and sandals, killing the fattened calf and having a celebratory feast.

But the parable does not end there. What of the older brother, symbol of the scribes and Pharisees who complain and are resentful about the seemingly charmed and privileged life of the prodigal? The older son is out in the fields working, doing the right thing. But when he nears the house and hears music and dancing, it does not seem to occur to him to share the joyful mood, to go in and see what the merriment is all about. Rather, aristocratically, he summons a servant for an explanation. The servant seems to lack all discretion and memory of what the older son is like and immediately spills out everything.

The righteous one is then angry. He won't go in.

But the father is the father of each son. Out he comes again, to plead. No embraces here. The righteous and the resentful do not seem to be into touch. The older son's speech is one of those literary masterpieces. It is a confession of the desperately good who are consumed with envy, who cannot face their shadow. His description of his brother, 'this son of yours' who has 'swallowed up your property' – and the Freudian touch – 'he and his women'… The brother complains that the father has not even offered him a kid to celebrate with his friends (what friends?) let alone the fattened calf. But he seems to be the type who would have put off the offer of any such gift to another time and conscientiously gone back to work.

The final quiet words of the father in the parable are tender words to the righteously hurt. 'My son, you are with me always and everything I have is yours' – not just property but the compassion of his forgiving heart. It was only right to rejoice when those who have strayed and sinned return and repent.

While this parable is classic, it also appears in other places in Luke, in encounters that Jesus experienced. A woman's version of the parable is found in 7:36-50, the story of the woman who was a sinner in the city. She is the prodigal. Simon the Pharisee and his guests are the older son. She is lavish in her tears of repentance, her expensive ointment and brushing Jesus' feet with her hair. Simon complains, 'if this man were a prophet he would know what kind of woman this is.' Jesus did know and could have quoted the story of the prophet Hosea and his love for Gomer, the temple prostitute, which became one of the key images of God's love for his people in the Jewish Scriptures. Jesus applauds her great love. She has sinned much and repented of much. She is beloved and forgiven.

A man's version is that of Zacchaeus, the tax-collector (19:1-10) the short man who climbed a tree, literally went out on a limb, 'branched out' to get a glimpse of Jesus. Once again there was complaint that Jesus ate with him. But Zacchaeus has sins of injustice to atone for. He will give half his property to the poor and will repay anybody he has cheated four times the amount. And Jesus can say that he has once again sought out the lost.

Emmaus

After the death of Jesus, the women go to the tomb as in the other Gospels, experience the emptiness of the tomb, hear the message of the two angels and tell the apostles what they heard. But to the apostles 'this story of theirs seemed pure nonsense, and they did not believe them' (24:11). The apostles in authority could not bring themselves to listen fully to the women and accept what they witnessed.

It is in this context that the principal Lukan resurrection story is told, 24:13-35, the two disciples and their encounter with Jesus on the road to Emmaus. The Lukan community has valued Jesus' encounters, as very personal encounters. These two disciples walking away from Jerusalem, their faces downcast, confess their dashed hopes to the stranger who joins them, who asks them what they are talking about and hears that they had had great hopes for Jesus and the revolution. They acknowledge that Jesus showed he was a prophet in all he said and did. But... Then they give their version of the women going to the tomb and not finding Jesus but declaring that they had seen a vision of angels. It is clear that they too have not been persuaded at all by the women.

Jesus' initial response would have given some joy to the women, 'You foolish men'. But he then shows them what the risen Christ can do, enlighten the listening mind as to the meaning of the suffering and death of Jesus. Jesus is the true servant who suffered for all but is now glorified. Listening to Jesus' words and being affected by their power moves them to invite him to stay with them. Then, as he eats with them, they recognise him as he repeats what he did at the Last Supper. They recognise him in the breaking of the bread. There is nowhere else to go but to rush back to Jerusalem with the good news.

The Gospel of Luke is a very warm Gospel, full of emotion. There are confrontations, but it is harmony and unity of spirit that are valued. Luke's is the Feeling Function Gospel. Reading it should be so personal that it has the effect that the two disciples felt on the road to Emmaus, 'did not our hearts burn within us as he talked to us on the road and explained the Scriptures to us?'

John's Gospel

The Gospel of John is the fourth and final Gospel. In fact, there were quite a number of 'Gospels' written in succeeding centuries, 'apocryphal gospels' attributed to a variety of authors like the apostle Thomas, but containing stories which are more like folklore than the stories of the authentic Gospels.

As with all generations and with many prayer movements today (and the Jesus-movies), people want to know more about Jesus' life. They want to know details. They want to know names. Many of the names of scriptural characters like Mary's parents, Joachim and Anne, like Dismas, the good thief, and like Longinus, the centurion who pierced Jesus' side, date from the second and third centuries. And they have passed into Christian folklore as if they were Gospel.

John's Gospel is not at all like this. Compiled, perhaps, by the last decade of the first century AD, it is more of a reflective, even mystical, Gospel. If the majority of early Christians, in Type statistical terms, identified with the Sensate Function then, as the first and second generations grew older, they seemed to respond more Intuitively to Jesus' story and John's Gospel emerges from this experience.

John's Gospel is complex, full of Intuitive connections. Our consideration of this Gospel reflects this Intuitive complexity.

The Johannine Community

American biblical scholar, Raymond Brown, in his 'Community of the Beloved Disciple', reminds us that the composition itself of the 'Johannine community' was quite complex and that the Gospel choices of stories pays compliment to the varying backgrounds of the groupings within the community. There were disciples of John the Baptist – and so there are many Baptist narratives. There were those influenced by such religious groups as the Essenes – and so there are passages incorporating their imagery and language, especially themes of light and darkness. There were Pharisees – and so, not only narratives critical of the Pharisees, but also the story of Nicodemus, the Pharisee who came by night to speak with Jesus and who took care of his burial. There were convert Samaritans – and so we have the story of the woman at the well. There were also Gnostics who questioned the physical reality of the incarnation of Jesus – and so we have, amongst other passages, the initial hymn to the Word and the declaration that the Word was made flesh (1:14) as well as doubting Thomas being invited to touch the wounds in Jesus' hands and side (20:24-29).

The Gospel seems to address itself to a wide spectrum of communities giving it a multi-layered texture eliciting a range of responses.

However, all the narratives and all the reflections are united in the aim of those who edited the stories, including those stories we have while dropping others:

> There were many other signs that Jesus worked and the disciples saw, but they are not recorded in this book. These are recorded so that you may believe that Jesus is the Christ, the Son of God, and that believing this you may have life through his name (20:30-31).

High Christology

The prologue to John, the hymn to the Word, declares that Jesus is the Word made flesh, 'the Son who is nearest to the

Father's heart and has made him known' (1:17). This initial acknowledgement that Jesus is the Word, the pre-existing Word made flesh, means that, unlike the Synoptics who incorporate a Low Christology, a portrait of Jesus that begins with his humanity and moves towards divinity, John's Gospel incorporates a High Christology, a portrait of Jesus which always presupposes his divinity.

This also means that readers of and listeners to this Gospel, especially in liturgy, have to respond on both levels. The Gospel is the story of Jesus of Nazareth, the man from Nazareth that people knew and communicated with at the human level. It is also the story of Jesus who is now known as the Risen Lord, the Word made flesh, one with the Father, whose divinity pervades all his sayings and all his actions. It is a more complex response than that to the Jesus of the Synoptics. This Johannine presentation of Jesus makes more intuitive demands on its readers.

Structure

The High Christology influences the structure of the Gospel. After the prologue and the preaching of John the Baptist (who is foreshadowed in the prologue) and Jesus' entry into ministry, announced by John, as well as his choosing of the initial disciples in chapter one, the chapters of the Gospel from 2-12 share a pattern. A story is told, a symbolic story, and there follows a meditative discourse on themes derived from the symbolic action. Sometimes the discourse occurs within the narrative, for instance, in the meeting with the woman of Samaria at the well (ch. 4) or in the healing of the man born blind (ch. 9). Chapter 13 also fits this pattern but it also serves as the opening of Jesus' passion or, in John's word, the 'hour' of exodus when Jesus goes from this world to the Father. In fact, there are three chapters of discourse, the Last Discourse, after the meal in the upper room and the washing of the disciples' feet (chs. 14-16). The discourse concludes with Jesus' prayer for unity (ch. 17).

John's Gospel has its distinctive passion narrative and its distinctive resurrection narratives. An appendix of resurrection stories comes in chapter 21 with the final comment:

> There were many other things that Jesus did; if all were written down, the world itself, I suppose, would not hold all the books that would have to be written (v. 24-25).

With Matthew's Gospel, the language tends to be 'no frills'. It is plain, clear and direct. John's Gospel, on the other hand, might be considered by some as quite prolix. It seems to enjoy words and phrases and their repetition. The discourses of the Gospel, especially the Last Discourse, have been likened to waves flowing on to the shore. The water comes in. Some of it remains, seeping into the sand. The rest is drawn out towards the sea again, only to be caught up in the next wave which rolls on to the sand, some of it remaining, seeping into the sand. The rest flows out towards the sea again. So, Jesus, in his words about remaining in his love, keeping his commandments, sending the Paraclete and being one with the Father, speaks like the waves rolling into the shore, making a point, returning to it while adding a little more. By the end of the discourse, Jesus' words pervade our consciousness without our necessarily being able to offer a concise quotation to sum everything up.

John and the Jewish Scriptures

While John, like Matthew, uses some fulfilment texts from the Jewish Scriptures, they are few in John compared with the number in Matthew's Gospel. The principal locus of fulfilment texts is the passion narrative in chapters 18-19: a quotation from Psalm 22:18 about the sharing of clothes and casting lots; from the same Psalm, 22:15, 'I am thirsty'; and, finally, two quotations when Jesus is pierced with a lance, an intuitively-combined quotation from Exodus 12:46 and Psalm 34:20 with reference to the Passover meal (Exodus) and the plight of the virtuous (Psalm 34) 'Not one bone of his will be broken' and another cross-referenced quotation, 'They shall look on the one whom they have pierced' (Zech12:10).

While the allusions to the Jewish Scriptures by John are intuitive, their introduction and observations after them are as precise as those of Matthew: with the clothes and the lots, 'In this way the words of Scripture were fulfilled... This is exactly what the soldiers did'; with Jesus' thirst, '...and to fulfil the Scriptures perfectly...'; with the piercing of Jesus' side, 'Because all this happened to fulfil the words of Scripture...'

However, John's references to the Jewish Scriptures are usually more complex. Jesus' words to the religious leaders after his cleansing of the Temple (2:13-25) are introduced by a fulfilment text, 'Then his disciples remembered the words of Scripture: Zeal for your house will devour me' (Ps 69:9).

When Jesus is asked for a sign, he answers, 'destroy this sanctuary and in three days I will raise it up.' His listeners take his words literally, thinking that he means the temple standing there before them in Jerusalem and they scoff referring to the forty-six years it took to build. John then takes readers to deeper meanings. 'He was speaking of the sanctuary that was his body.' The theme of the building and the dedication of the temple and the entry of the glory cloud in the books of the Kings, the pervading pagan practices and the loss of the glory cloud as well as its later return and the building of the new temple in the prophet

Ezekiel, and temple pilgrimage prayers and hymns in the psalms, is well developed. The temple is not only the home of God, it is a guarantee of God's presence. It is the sacrament of God's presence. The glory cloud of God descended into the temple at its dedication (1 Kings 8:10-13); the glory cloud left the temple and went into exile with the people when those in Jerusalem were unfaithful to the covenant (Ezek 10:18-22); it returned from exile with the people (Ezek 43:1-12). By identifying with the temple, Jesus makes great claims.

But, the Gospel goes on to say, his disciples remembered what he said after his resurrection from the dead and they believed the Scriptures and the words he had said. Another reason for remembering those words was Jesus being pierced on Calvary. His body, the temple, was pierced in the side with a lance and immediately blood and water flowed out (19:31-37). After the exile, the prophet Ezekiel had a vision of the new temple (ch. 47). From its side saving and cleansing water flowed, up to the prophet's ankles, then to his knees, to his waist and so abundantly that he was not able to cross. Through these references to the theme of the temple, the Gospel establishes the meaning of Jesus and his mission.

While on this Intuitive theme, it should be pointed out that Jesus is described in intuitive terms, 'Jesus knew them all and did not trust himself to them; he never needed evidence about anyone; he could tell what a person had in them' (2:24-25).

The woman caught in the very act of committing adultery (8:1-11) is a favourite for homilies (and the joke about Jesus telling his mother to stop throwing stones when he invites whoever is without guilt...). However, most scholars suggest that it is more likely of Synoptic origin (Lukan in character, some say) rather than Johannine. But it does offer an interesting parallel with the Jewish Scriptures, or a passage, originally written in Greek, which is not considered part of the Jewish canon. It is the tale of Susanna and the elders (Dan 13).

In the original story, Susanna is innocent yet condemned by the guilty religious leaders. Daniel, with some basic forensic astuteness, disproves their story and Susanna is vindicated. In the Gospel story, the woman is guilty and accused by the religious leaders who are presumed innocent. Jesus challenges the leaders with seeming nonchalance, and the woman is left alone, freed by Jesus. She is not condemned by Jesus. He lets her go, urging her (without guarantee) not to repeat what she has done, and to sin no more.

Daniel was a great figure but, as in Matthew's Gospel, a greater than... a greater than Daniel is here.

Yet another way that John's Gospel uses the Jewish Scriptures is by way of a sacred pun. Scholars remind us that a pun, impossible to reproduce in English, is at the core of the meaning of John's Gospel. The Hebrew word for lamb is 'ebed'. The Hebrew word for servant is 'eben'. When John the Baptist points out the lamb of God who takes away the sin of the world, there is the allusion to the lamb-servant, the lamb of Isaiah 53 who is led to the slaughter bearing our sins and by whose punishment we are healed. Jesus is the servant of Isaiah in going to his death. After his scourging and torment, Pilate alludes, 'Behold the man', to the words of the servant song:

> without beauty, without majesty we saw him,
> no looks to attract our eyes,
> a thing despised and rejected,
> a man of sorrows and familiar with suffering,
> a man to make people screen their faces (Is 53:2-3).

And, according to John, Jesus died on the cross at the same moment as the passover lambs were slaughtered, not one of whose bones was to be broken.

All the Gospels have good shepherd parables, especially

Matthew, with not only the lost sheep but also the last judgement. All these elements of sheep and shepherd imagery are gathered together in Ezekiel 34. John gives a more meditative turn to the shepherd imagery. Jesus is the good shepherd. The good shepherd is the principal parable in John's Gospel (10:1-5). After the brief narrative, the discourse on the meaning of the shepherd is introduced by another theme of the Gospel, the inability of those listening to really understand what he is saying. Jesus uses the Ezekiel images in his discourse but, by the end of the discourse, he has led his listeners back to the theme of his being one with the Father.

John's Gospel uses the richness of the heritage of the Jewish Scriptures, but the reader must work to appreciate and understand.

Signs and Wonders

There are miracles in John's Gospel, especially the unique story of the wedding feast at Cana, but they are not numerous: the official's son (ch. 4), the lame man at the pool (ch. 5), the feeding of the thousands (ch. 6), the man born blind (ch. 9) and the raising of Lazarus (ch. 11). But the miracle aspect is of least interest to the Gospel. These stories are important as 'signs and wonders'. From the book of Isaiah with its references to wonderful healings – the blind seeing, deaf hearing, the lame walking – through the healings of Elijah and Elisha, God's special presence was to be heralded by these wonders. But the wonders were also 'signs'. We would say that they were symbols. They did not merely point out Jesus as someone who was bringing God's healing presence, the stories themselves had significant meanings of abundance: wine or bread, sight to see the light of the world and recovery, even from death, to experience resurrection.

This theme of signs is introduced early in the Gospel, after the wedding feast, as the deeper reason for the changing of water into wine: 'This was the first of the signs given by Jesus: it was given at Cana in Galilee. He let his glory be seen, and his disciples believed in him' (2:11-2). The cure of the nobleman's son (4:43-54) gives the occasion for Jesus to elaborate on this manifestation of glory and eliciting of belief. Jesus says, 'So you will not believe unless you see signs and portents', unusual events rather than the wonders which manifest God's presence. But the nobleman has faith and his son is healed. 'He and all his household believed.' The narrative ends with, 'This was the second sign given by Jesus, on his return from Judaea to Galilee.'

The religious leaders in the temple asked Jesus for a sign. He offered them his temple, his body, as the sign. The disciples would later remember this and believe. The water given to Jesus by the woman at the well is a sign of living water. The bread that was multiplied in abundance is a sign of the bread of life. Lazarus' new life is a sign of the resurrection.

Johannine Theology

The structure of sign narrative followed by reflective discourse means that most of the chapters of the Gospel are units in themselves with a unified theme. This is most evident in chapter 6, one of the longest chapters in the whole of the New Testament.

The chapter begins with a sign and wonder. And it is given a symbolic setting, one of the Feasts which John's Gospel sees as so important, 'It was shortly before the Jewish feast of Passover' (v. 4). It also reminds us that this is no ordinary narrative; there is a background of High Christology, 'Jesus said this (asking where to buy bread for the crowd) only to test Philip; he himself knew exactly what he was going to do' (v. 7). The miracle of the loaves and the abundance of the leftovers proceeds along the familiar lines of the Synoptic accounts.

But this is a sign and, as so often happens, it is misinterpreted by those who see it. It does not elicit faith – although they recognise Jesus as 'the prophet who is to come into the world'. Rather, the crowds are so impressed by what Jesus has done that they want to make him king (and Jesus' later words to Pilate indicate how he perceived himself in the role of king (18:33-40)).

There follows John's version of the storm on the lake, this time Jesus walking on the water and his reassurance that they should not be afraid (v. 16-21). With the arrival of Jesus at Capernaum, he begins a discourse on the bread of life.

It opens with Jesus having more to say about signs, that the crowds had missed the meaning of the sign and were merely wanting more free bread. He tries to take them further into an understanding of who he was and what he was offering through himself, the bread of life: eternal life. But the crowds are still stuck on the role of signs. They even now ask Jesus for a sign. He takes them back to the Exodus story and the occasion, in the book of Numbers, where they had manna to eat in the desert. Having established the link between their ancestors and themselves, between God feeding them with a wonderful bread in the desert and God now giving them the bread of life, Jesus himself, he is ready to explore some meanings of the gift of eternal life.

The chapter is structured well, with Jesus speaking and then a break coming with the response of the crowd. By verse 41, it is clear that many cannot recognise the sign at all, able only to stay literally with bread, complaining about Jesus' credentials. By verse 52, they have begun to understand something of what Jesus is getting at but stay stuck on a literal use of the word, 'flesh'. By verse 59, it has become intolerable teaching to some, frighteningly literal. Jesus tells them that his words are 'spiritual'.

At the end of the narrative, just as at the beginning, the High Christology is referred to, 'Jesus knew from the outset those who did not believe, and who it was who would betray him' (v. 64). The testing of belief in response to the sign is finally encapsulated in his close group of disciples with Judas failing the test of belief (as he would when Mary pours the lavish ointment on Jesus (12:1-8)), at the Last Supper where he leaves the upper room and it is night (13:30) and in the garden (18:5)), and with Peter responding in the words of faith, 'Lord, who shall we go to? You have the message of eternal life, and we believe; we know that you are the Holy One of God' (v. 68-69).

Chapter 6 contains a theology of Eucharist as a sign and wonder, a sign, bread of life, that should elicit belief. However, the chapter also makes explicit a theology of what we call 'grace', that God does the choosing and we respond in faith. This has always been a problem, how to express the experience of faith: God taking the initiative or our taking the first step in freedom to assent in faith? It was the conflict between Augustine and Pelagius. It is the perennial problem of most people talking like Pelagius, that our response in grace depends on us. However, Jesus uses the language of attraction in John 6. God is so loving that we are drawn towards God and in that gracious attraction, we are graced and respond in faith (v. 44).

This chapter also develops the theology of the relationship between Jesus and the Father, their unity which is repeated so often during the Gospel, the unity into which all people are to be drawn if they are chosen, not as servants but as friends, if they keep Jesus' commandment of love and allow the Spirit to remind them of all that Jesus said and did.

The phrase that the Gospel puts into the mouth of Jesus with all his signs, the water, the bread, the light, the resurrection and the life, is 'I am', recalling the name that God gave to Moses, the living God, by which name all generations were to call God (Ex 3).

'Eternal Life' is the phrase used throughout the Gospel to encompass this theology. Its most succinct expression is found in 17:3. '... you let him give eternal life to all those you have entrusted to him. And eternal life is this: to know and love you, the only true God and Jesus Christ whom you have sent.'

Jesus' Hour

Perhaps a useful way of showing the Intuitive perspective of John's Gospel is by tracing a theme through the Gospel, seeing how it threads but, as it threads, it develops more and more nuances until, by the death of Jesus, it can be seen as an all-pervading theme.

The origin of the theme in the Jewish Scriptures is the prophetic theme of 'The Day of the Lord'. In the prophet Amos, for instance, the Day of the Lord is one of darkness and doom. It is a day of judgement for those who have not been faithful to the covenant. However, it is not a day of complete despair. For those who remain, repent and turn again to the covenant, it is a day of salvation. Other prophets, like Isaiah, developed this theme of the remnant, using images like the vine tended by the vinekeeper (ch. 5). The destruction of Samaria and the northern kingdom of Israel (722-1 BC) and the subsequent deportations, followed later by the destruction of Jerusalem (587 BC) with the destruction of the Temple and the exile of the people, showed that the worst could happen.

The Synoptics introduce the ministry of Jesus as a new return from exile, with highways made through the desert.

In John, the Day of the Lord is the 'hour', the special time for God's justice and salvation, and it is achieved in Jesus.

The first mention of the hour is in chapter 2 at Cana. Jesus declines his mother's invitation to help the bride and groom and their guests as his 'hour had not yet come'. However, he does relent and, in the symbolic setting of marriage – Pauline literature, especially Ephesians 5, likes to speak of the relationship between Jesus and the Church in marriage imagery – and with water (baptismal) and wine (eucharistic), he offers the first sign, letting his glory be revealed for a response of faith. It is in all these senses that Cana is an anticipation of the hour on Calvary.

However, with the themes of the hour and of the glory established, another theme is introduced in chapter 3. It concerns Jesus being 'lifted up'. In Jesus' conversation with Nicodemus, he alludes to the image of Moses setting up bronzed serpents on crosses as signs of God's healing promise so that all who gazed on the serpents would regain their health and would live.

> ... the Son of Man must be lifted up
> as Moses lifted up the serpent in the desert.
> so that everyone who believes may have
>   eternal life in him.
>
> Yes, God loved the world so much
> that he gave his only Son,
> so that everyone who believes in him
>   may not be lost
> but may have eternal life (3:13-16).

The hour and the glory are associated now with eternal life. This will all happen when Jesus is lifted up. There are two other discourses in which Jesus refers to his being lifted up. In 12:32, Jesus anticipates his crucifixion and adds another feature to the lifting up. He says:

And when I am lifted up from the earth,
I shall draw all people to myself.

And the narrative adds: 'By these words he indicated the kind of death he would die.' Jesus, at the hour, is lifted up and, arms outstretched, draws all people to himself. The purpose of the being lifted up and drawing all people to himself is made clear in 8:28:

When you have lifted up the Son of Man,
then you will know that I am he.

This means that at the hour, on the cross, Jesus will be revealed as one with the Father, one with 'I AM', the living God. Again in chapter 12, this whole experience of Jesus is one of glory. Just as at Cana, he let his glory be seen, so this hour is the hour of glory:

Now the hour has come
for the Son of Man to be glorified (v. 23).

Jesus amplifies this with the well-known parable: 'Unless a wheat grain falls on the ground and dies, it remains only a single grain; but if it dies, it yields a rich harvest. Anyone who loves their life, loses it; anyone who hates their life in this world will keep it for the eternal life' (v. 24-25).

The introduction to the Last Supper (13:1) states that Jesus' hour is his death, a symbolic Passover death. The motivation of the death is love… 'but now he showed how perfect his love was'. He washed the disciples' feet, a prophetic symbolic action of the master as servant, giving a new commandment for a new covenant people, 'Love one another; just as I have loved you, you must also love one another' (v. 34). 'By this love you have for one another, everyone will know that you are my disciples' (v. 35). Jesus' testament at this hour is the new commandment of love. All disciples will love as Jesus did, thus glorifying God, revealing God and inviting all people to eternal life.

During the Last Discourse, Jesus will call himself the Way, the Truth and the Life (14:6), and he will remind his disciples that they are no longer servants but friends and there is no greater love than laying down one's life for one's friends (15:9-17).

On Calvary, John's Gospel presents us with an intimate tableau. Near the cross of Jesus stood his mother. He had anticipated revealing this final glory at her request at Cana. Now she shares in the hour. Mary, who like the prophets said 'yes' to God's word and gave birth to God's Word, is the prophet at the foot of the cross. The disciple Jesus loved also stands there, the friend who is also apostle of the good news of eternal life. Popular piety of crucifixes often has Mary Magdalene kneeling at the foot of the cross between Mary and the beloved disciple. Mary Magdalene, seen through the Hosea tradition of the shrine prostitute who leaves her husband but who returns to his love, represents sinful Israel, sinful people, the image of the 'beloved and forgiven' (19:25-27).

This weaving of threads through the Gospel, the threads of the hour, the glory, the lifting up, the drawing all to himself, the revelation that I am He, comes together in the image of Jesus dying on the cross. It is not so much an agonising Jesus on the cross, although he does say 'I am thirsty' and takes the vinegar offered him. Rather, it is a glorious Jesus, anticipating resurrection. Jesus on the cross is one with the Father. Everyone should be able to see this. All is accomplished and, bowing his head, Jesus gives up his Spirit. This is, in retrospect, a 'glorious' image of the Trinity: the Son, one with the Father, breathing out the Spirit.

Jesus, the Passover servant-lamb, is dead and will be buried. Blood and water, as in Ezekiel's image of the temple, flow from his side. The First Letter of John (5:7-8) mystically speaks of Jesus coming by the water, the blood and the spirit. For the Hebrews, the life was seen as in the blood. Jesus poured out his life as the blood flowed from his pierced side. For Ezekiel, the cleansing and refreshing water that readied the people for the new heart of flesh by which they would know how to love God and be a covenant people was filled with God's spirit, the spirit of creation and new creation. The First Letter of John says that the blood, the water and the Spirit all witness to who Jesus was and what he accomplished.

Resurrection Stories

While the death of Jesus in John is practically a resurrection story – Jesus, in his final yes to the Father gives himself so completely that the Father can do nothing else but respond in lovingly receiving his yes and loving Jesus into new, risen life – the final narratives are testimony to the risen Jesus. Testimony, truthful witness, is a strong theme of the Gospel. What is unusual about the Johannine resurrection stories is that it is the specially chosen friends who are depicted as hesitant and slow to believe. The disciple Jesus loved outran Peter to the tomb. They do not see Jesus. They look into the tomb and the disciple Jesus loved believes, but 'till this moment they had failed to understand the teaching of Scripture, that he must rise from the dead' (20:1-10).

While Jesus breathes his spirit on them and gives them his peace, Thomas is absent and doubts. The dramatic story of Jesus coming again to the disciples and his appeal to Thomas has as its climax, 'Doubt no longer but believe' (20:28). Thomas can now say, 'My Lord and my God', but Jesus' response is a word of encouragement for the later generations of the Church, for the Johannine community:

> You believe because you can see me.
> Happy are those who have not seen and yet believe (20:29).

The person who does see, however, is Mary Magdalene, the beloved and forgiven sinner at the foot of the cross. Her actions and her words, her seeking her beloved, echo the Song of Songs (3:1-3). The sinful prostitute has now become the beloved. Jesus calls her by name and she can recognise him. It is Mary who is commissioned by the Risen Lord to explain the completion of his mission to the men, to his brothers. She is the first witness to the Resurrection and the first with a mission from the Risen Lord, an apostle. (Has this been explored fully enough for its repercussions on the roles of men and women in the Church today?)

The Gospel of John has always been considered as mystical, symbolic, always complex. An Intuitive Gospel.

Jesus, our Spirituality and Type

In reflecting on the Gospels and how they can be read with the insights of Type, we appreciate that they offer portraits of Jesus that are consistent with the perceptions of Type. This can lead to a deepening of our spirituality and prayerful response to Jesus according to our Type, as well as a challenge to go where, of ourselves, we are not able, to the revelation of a Jesus opposite to our Type, a Jesus we surrender to.

As was said at the beginning of this book, Paul urges the Philippians and us, 'In your minds you must be the same as Christ Jesus.' In recognising how we are particularly gifted and graced by God in our minds and in our hearts, especially in the 'Functions' that Psychological Type theory open up to us, we find a way of recognising Jesus and recognising ourselves.

For most of us, it will be in reflecting on Jesus' way of being Intuitive or Sensate, Thinking or Feeling, that we can experience something of the 'sameness'. It is said, traditionally that 'Grace builds on Nature'. The prayerful reflection on, and the imitation in action of the 'sameness' is one of the graced ways of building on nature.

The author of *The Spiritual Exercises*, Ignatius Loyola described a very sensate way of prayer. He urged retreatants to enter into the Gospel picture, to be there, noticing the detail of the picture, finding where they chose to be in that situation (near to Jesus or more distant), to live the Gospel incident, to be amongst the Twelve when Jesus healed the leper, to be on the mountain with Peter, James and John seeing Jesus transfigured, to stand at the foot of the cross on Calvary with Jesus' mother, Mary.

The mystical writer of the same 16th century as Ignatius, and also Spanish, Teresa of Avila, acknowledged that there were many rooms of prayer in the Interior Castle, but that the more deeply one was led into the centre of the Castle, the more one had to let go of attachments to the comforting experiences of prayer and surrender oneself to the experience of the unknown God. Her later contemporary and friend, John of the Cross, wrote of these surrenders and of their uncertainty and pain, calling them 'the Dark Night of the Senses' and 'the Dark Night of the Soul'.

While this is too much of a generalisation, it is still useful to remark that Ignatius of Loyola's prayer corresponds to (at least initial) sensate experience of Jesus, while that of Teresa and John of the Cross corresponds to something of intuitive prayer.

In the language of Type, we need to appreciate what our most familiar and Dominant Function is so that we can be graced there. We are also graced in our Auxiliary Function (remembering, of course, that very few people live from an exact textbook outline and that our spiritual journey is not to be lived from a schematic straitjacket).

However, Type theory reminds us that our Tertiary Function and, especially, our Inferior Function are in the realm of shadow, that they need to be developed for wholeness, but that they are not usually exercised with ease or with a quick decision of our will.

Type theory meets theory of the growth of the spiritual life here. The ascetic phrase, *'Agere contra'*, to try 'to act against oneself', also has a long tradition. In Type terms, we might say that it is urging us to our opposite Functions, to surrender to ways of prayer that do not come naturally, that we are to be led by God and grace.

This, of course, means that the Intuitive is led into a simpler and more focused prayer; that the Sensate is led into a realm of undreamed of possibilities in prayer.

As regards the Gospels, it means that the Sensate, who may identify with the Jesus of Mark, is drawn to the mystical Jesus of John. And, of course, vice versa, the Intuitive, at home in John's Gospel, is drawn into the 'real' and detailed life of Jesus of Mark's Gospel. The Thinker who appreciates the clarity and objectivity of Matthew is to be drawn to the personalised stories of Luke's Gospel while the Feeler at home with Luke and his cast of loved characters has to move to the clear-eyed teaching of Matthew's Gospel.

Individuals know the ways that they are drawn in prayer and in the realities of their day-by-day life, so it is not my role to repeat what the increasing library of book and articles on Type and Prayer have said. 'From Image to Likeness' remains one of the best studies of Jesus, Type and prayer and I would urge readers to learn from it. Rather, my task has been to highlight the perspectives of each Gospel and its portrait of Jesus. This, I hope, offers some light for prayer.

Matthew's Jesus

The Jesus who emerges from Matthew's Gospel is a strong Jesus, sometimes a stern Jesus, a Jesus of principle. One can call him a 'Thinking Function Jesus'. Of course, the Jesus of Matthew's community exhibits a Feeling Function, but the thinking seems more dominant.

The word to focus our attention on the Jesus of Matthew is 'authority'. The people are in admiration of him when they listen to his teaching, especially after the Sermon on the Mount. 'His teaching made a deep impression on the people, because he taught them with authority and not like their own scribes' (7:28-9).

The initial presentation of Jesus is as the fulfilment of prophecy and of the hopes of the people of Israel. He is the authentic Son of David (1:1-17). He is Emmanuel, God-with-us (1:23). He is the infant king of the Jews (2:2) to be worshipped by the wise visitors from the East. He is Herod's victim called, like his ancestors, out of Egypt (2:13-15). He settles in Nazareth, foster son of Joseph and son of Mary (2:21-23). Matthew's Gospel tells us who Jesus is, his importance, and the reasons for it.

The first words of Jesus in Matthew's Gospel are distinctive. John the Baptist wants to be baptised by Jesus. Jesus says, 'Leave it like this for the time being; it is fitting that we should, in this way, do all that righteousness demands' (3:15). Jesus is a man who does what is right and what is fitting. This is clear in his biblical responses to Satan during the temptations (4:1-11). And the only words that he speaks prior to the Sermon on the Mount (where he does speak for three chapters) are: 'Repent, for the kingdom of heaven is close at hand' (4:17) and to Peter and Andrew,

'Follow me and I will make you fishers of people' (4:19).

Jesus does not waste words. He is clear and succinct. Some of the strongest memories of Jesus in Christian culture and beyond it are words from the Sermon on the Mount. There is the plain profoundness of the Beatitudes (5:1-12), the utmost respect for the Law and its commandments and the raising of moral standards: not merely the forbidding of killing but of calling anyone fool; not merely the forbidding of adultery but of lustful intentions. Integrity means plain authenticity, 'all you need say is 'Yes' if you mean yes, 'No' if you mean no'.

It is no longer an eye for an eye, a tooth for a tooth, but turning the other cheek. It is no longer merely loving neighbour but loving enemy as well. And the appeal for these principles is that this is what God is like, 'be perfect just as your heavenly Father is perfect' (5:20-48). (It is interesting that Luke replaces the word 'perfect' with 'merciful' (6:36).)

Jesus is close to the Father and speaks of him intimately. The God who sees what we do in secret will reward private prayer, fasting and almsgiving. Parading ourselves and trumpeting our good deeds has no place in Jesus' codes of religious behaviour. The Lord's prayer is given as an alternative to pagan babbling. 'Where your treasure is, there will your heart be too' (6:21). Jesus mellows a little in his quite stark teaching of values to rely on images for trust in the providence of God: the birds of the air and the lilies of the field (6:25-34). Jesus is no starry-eyed optimist, 'So do not worry about tomorrow: tomorrow will take care of itself, each day has enough trouble of its own' (6:34).

The third chapter of the Sermon on the Mount also has teaching that is always quoted with authority: 'Do not judge, and you will not be judged' (7:1); 'Hypocrite, take the plank out of your own eye first, and then you will see clearly enough to take the splinter out of your brother's (or sister's) eye' (7:5); and the Golden Rule, 'So always treat others as you would like them to treat you' (7:12).

The Sermon concludes with the parable of the house built on sand which collapsed and the house built on rock which withstood the gales (7:24-27). And the mark of the true disciple? 'It is not those who say to me 'Lord, Lord', who will enter the kingdom of heaven, but the person who does the will of my Father in heaven' (7:21).

Jesus is also a straight talker. His encounter with the centurion and his amazement at his faith (8:5-13) is soon followed by strong words on the absolute nature of discipleship, 'leave the dead to bury their dead'. And, then comes the storm on the lake, 'Why are you so frightened, you men of little faith?' (8:26).

Jesus is also laconic. To the devils going into the Gadarene swine, 'Go then' (8:32). To Matthew, 'Follow me' (9:9).

And he confronts. To those who were criticising him for forgiving the paralytic, 'Why do you have such wicked thoughts in your hearts...?' (9:4). It is strongly present in the 'Apostolic Discourse' of chapter 10. If the disciples are not received well, they should shake the dust from their feet (10:15). He speaks of betrayal within families and urges fidelity and trust that the spirit will guide what the persecuted have to say (10:17-33). 'But the one who disowns me in the presence of people, I will disown in the presence of my Father in heaven' (10:33). He has come, not to bring peace, but a sword (10:34). 'Anyone who does not take up the cross and follow in my footsteps is not worthy of me. Whoever finds their life will lose it; whoever loses their life for my sake will find it' (10:39). Chorazin and Bethsaida, cities of Galilee where he preached, are condemned for their faithlessness. Judgement day will be harder for them than for Sodom (11:20-24).

There is much discussion about evil spirits, that blasphemy against the Holy Spirit can never be forgiven

(12:22-32). There are condemnations of the evil of the religious leaders of the day, which reaches a rhetorical peak in chapter 23, 'Woe to you, scribes and Pharisees…'.

Of course, there are sayings that are 'softer': Jesus sorry for the crowds that are harassed and like sheep without a shepherd (9:36); the reward for those who give a cup of cold water to the little ones (10:42); and, most significant of all, his prayer to the Father about hiding things from the learned and the clever and revealing them to mere children, followed by the invitation to come to him when overburdened and he will give rest because he is gentle and humble of heart (11:25-30).

With parables, their recounting is, at first (ch. 13), generally plain. These are the parables of the kingdom. The parables of justice are more developed but retain their straight tone and a touch of severity. People are condemned for their behaviour: the unforgiving debtor (18:23-35), the grumbling labourers in the vineyard (20:1-16), the son who said he would go to work and didn't (21:28-32), the wicked tenants who killed the son of the owner of the vineyard (21:33-42), the guest without the wedding garment (22:1-14), the foolish bridesmaids (25:1-13), the good-for-nothing servant who buried the talent (25:14-30) and the people at the judgement who have shown no charity (25:31-46). There is language of prison, exterior darkness and eternal punishment.

Peter figures a great deal in Matthew's Gospel. Jesus has called him from his fishing. Peter shares in the enthusiasm of the other disciples but he is also an apostle, one of the Twelve, named first. He was amongst those in the boat during the storm who were afraid. On the lake he wanted to walk on the water, but he wavered and doubted and sank (14:22-33). Each time, the rebuke concerns 'little faith'. Yet, it is Peter who speaks up when Jesus asks what people are saying about him and who they think he is (16:13-20). 'You are the Christ, the Son of the Living God.' Peter, the

Rock on which the Church is built, then receives the keys of the kingdom and the power to bind and loose.

But only two verses later, Peter, in his earnestness, wants to save Jesus from suffering and is rebuked as a Satan, an obstacle in Jesus' path, not thinking in God's way (16:21-3).

Then, six days later, Peter, James and John experience the transfiguration of Jesus, and Peter, in his enthusiasm, wants to make tents for them to stay there on the mountain (17:1-8).

It is Peter who is asked about the shekel tax – and Jesus pays it for him. It is Peter who asks Jesus about the extent of forgiveness, 'As often as seven times?' (18:21-22). He also asks about what reward there is for the disciples who had left everything to follow Jesus. Jesus promises a hundredfold in this life and eternal life in the next (19:27-29).

Yet, it is Peter who proclaims that he will never deny Jesus, 'Even if I have to die with you, I will never disown you'(26:30-35) but he denies Jesus spectacularly (26:69-75). Peter seems to be Jesus' closest friend in Matthew's Gospel. But it is an up-and-down friendship. This Gospel is not the best source for studying Jesus' friendships.

Before Matthew's account of the passion, there is the eschatological discourse, Jesus using dramatic, picturesque language and images to heighten the sense that he is the fulfilment of all prophecy and that his death will bring on the last fatal times – which may also be a time of salvation.

While the account of the passion is similar to those of the other Gospels, there are many distinctive features. As Jesus, at the beginning of the Gospel, is to be understood in the light of the Jewish Scriptures, so also at the end. But he is also to be understood in the politics of the time, of the clash between the Jews and Rome, specifically between the religious leaders and Pontius Pilate.

It is only in Matthew that we read such a vivid account of Judas filled with remorse at his betrayal of Jesus and flinging the thirty pieces of silver at the chief priest and elders before hanging himself (27:3-10). It is only in Matthew that Pilate is warned by his wife not to have anything to do with Jesus' death (27:19); only in Matthew that there is considerable discussion after Jesus' death between the chief priests and Pharisees, discussing with Pilate Jesus' talk of rising after three days and asking Pilate to ensure security against the stealing of the body (27:62-6). And they bribe the soldiers to keep the information about the empty tomb quiet and spread the rumour (that still persisted to the time of the writing of the Gospel) that the disciples had stolen the body.

Matthew's Gospel ends with Jesus' own words. He speaks, as always, with authority and commissions his disciples to preach, baptise and teach observance of all the commandments that he had given them.

Jesus is faithful. He will be with them always, to the end of time.

Mark's Jesus

Jesus is presented quite clearly in the Gospel of Mark as the Son of God, not the divine Jesus that he was later perceived to be, but rather the special Son of God who was to fulfil all prophecy and be the Servant-Saviour-Son of Man. The presentation of Jesus and the Jesus who emerges can be described as 'Sensate'.

Jesus is described as growing into his being the Son of God, step by step, from initially not wanting anything of his reputation to be talked about – even though, despite his warnings, his reputation spread rapidly – but gradually coming into a sense of who he was and was called to be. When this happens, he is ready to go to his passion and death.

This occurs at the beginning of his ministry when he submits to John's baptism. It is presented almost as an anointing of him as the servant, the beloved of God on whom God's Spirit rests (1:9-11). In the strength of this announcement Jesus is drawn into the desert for forty days of retreat and temptation (like Israel of old for forty years in the desert) and is ready to begin his ministry (1:12-30).

The Jesus of Mark is sketched in brief episodes. At times, the Gospel gives us only the bare outline of Jesus' ministry. Although, as the Gospel proceeds, some of the narratives get longer. But, even in the passion account, the episodes are quite brief. Jesus tends to speak briefly and clearly. He acts directly.

> After John had been arrested, Jesus went into Galilee. There he proclaimed the Good News from God. 'The time has come' he said, 'and the kingdom of God is close at hand. Repent and believe the Good News' (1:14-15).

Jesus is on his way.

So it is in the description of the facts/events that Jesus is encountered rather than in the development of the meanings of the events, as occurs in John. The events are the basis for the meanings that the Markan community will be able to develop and understand.

The Jesus of Mark is a man who is touched by people and who touches them. When he was told of Peter's mother-in-law being ill, he straightaway went to her, 'took her by the hand and helped her up' (2:31).

When the leper broke the law in coming to Jesus to be healed, Jesus is described as being moved with compassion and 'stretched out his hand and touched him' (1:41). Not only was there a personal risk in touching the leper, there was the legal risk, with Jesus technically being leper for thirty days and having to remain on the margins in quarantine (1:45).

It is in the episode of the healing of the woman with the haemorrhage that a more mysterious dimension of the touching of Jesus comes to the fore. When Jesus is touched in faith, simply the touching of his cloak, he is 'immediately aware that power had gone out from him' (5:30). The power had gone out from him to her with the effect of instant drying up of her bleeding. When he heals it is as if Jesus loses something of himself. In giving, he gives something of himself. But, in return, he has received the faith of the person requesting the healing. 'My daughter, your faith has restored you to health' (5:34).

Jesus then proceeds to the house of Jairus and takes his daughter by the hand. Speaking in Aramaic, he tells her to get up. When she is walking around, he tells the parents to give her something to eat (5:40-43).

In a miracle exclusive (in its detail) to Mark (7:31-37), people bring 'a deaf man with an impediment in his speech' to Jesus to be healed. They want Jesus to lay his hand on the man. Still reserved, Jesus takes the man way from the crowd, privately, and actually puts his fingers into the man's ears and touches his tongue with spittle. There is further Sensate description of this healing. When Jesus looks up to heaven, he sighs. Then, as with the daughter of Jairus, he speaks in Aramaic, 'Ephphatha' ('Be opened'). The description of what happens to the deaf man with the impediment in his speech includes his ears being opened, the ligament of his tongue being loosened and his speaking clearly.

The healing of the youth who seems to be epileptic but is interpreted as having a devil in him, is described in Mark's Gospel (9:14-29) in far more detail than in the versions in Matthew and Luke. We are just over the midway point of the Gospel. Jesus' reputation is stronger than ever and he does not seem to be asking people to be quiet about who he is. He is much more evidently the Son of God. He preaches the kingdom and repentance. He mixes comfortably with sinners and draws them to him. He speaks with authority with the religious leaders. He teaches in parables. He has healed many who were suffering with many different illnesses.

Now, as Jesus comes down the mountain from the privileged experience for Peter, James and John, his transfiguration, and they are discussing the current question about the coming of Elijah, he rejoins the disciples. 'The moment they saw him the whole crowd were struck with amazement and ran to greet him.' A desperate father describes the symptoms of his son's illness. 'There is a spirit of dumbness in him and when it takes hold of him it throws him to the ground, and he foams at the mouth, grinds his teeth and goes rigid' (v. 18). The disciples are unable to cast the devil out. When the boy is brought to Jesus, he again has convulsions, foams at the mouth, falls to the ground and lies writhing there (v. 20-21).

Jesus takes the opportunity to teach the crowd how faith is needed for any healing. 'I do have faith. Help the little faith I have', says the father (v. 25). After Jesus rebukes the spirit in the boy and he convulses yet again with the spirit shouting as it comes out of him, the boy lies on the ground 'so like a corpse that most of them said, 'he is dead'' (v. 26). But, as so often, Jesus took him by the hand and helped him up, and he was able to stand (v. 27).

It is not only on the occasion of a healing that Jesus touches. 'People were bringing little children to him, for him to touch them' (10:13). The disciples are still obtuse and they turn the children and the people away. This reaction of the disciples certainly touches Jesus interiorly, and not with compassion. He is indignant but he invites the children to come to him. He uses the situation to say that discipleship means being like a little child and the kingdom of God belongs to them (10:14-15). And he does touch them. 'He put his arms round them, laid his hands on them and gave them his blessing' (10:16).

Jesus as teacher in Mark is also brief and direct. There are comparatively fewer parables. The parable of the sower has a pride of place along with its explanation and some more succinct parables of the kingdom (4:1-34).

Each of the three Gospels has condemnations of the Pharisees and their hypocrisy. Mark's three verses (12:38-40) serve as a precis of the others. He includes the walking about in long robes, the being greeted obsequiously in the market-places, the taking of front seats in the synagogues and the places of honour at banquets. They are then condemned as swallowing up the property of widows while making a show of lengthy prayers. And, then, the verdict, 'the more severe will be the sentence they receive'.

Another teaching passage common to the Synoptics is the discussion with the Sadducees about the after-life, the episode where they elaborate the story of the woman whose seven husbands die, in order to ridicule the idea of heaven. Luke's more personal approach has some of the scribes praising Jesus for his wisdom, 'well put, Master' (20:27-40). Matthew, on the other hand, concludes the narrative with a return to his theme of Jesus and his authority and the impact that it made on the people, 'And his teaching made a deep impression on the people who heard it' (22:23-33).

Mark's version is quite similar to those of Matthew and Luke. But he simply concludes the narrative, 'You are very much mistaken' (12:27).

It is the same with the account of the passion. The episodes are generally brief and direct. Again, the detail is the strength of the narrative's impact. 'Some of them started spitting at him and, blindfolding him, began hitting him with their fists and shouting, 'Play the prophet!' And the attendants rained blows on him' (14:65). Peter denies Jesus, 'calling down curses on himself and swearing'. The cock crows the second time. 'And he burst into tears' (14:66-72).

> The soldiers led him away to the inner part of the palace, that is, the Praetorium, and called the whole cohort together. They dressed him up in purple, twisted some thorns into a crown and put it on him. And they began saluting him, 'Hail, king of the Jews!' They struck his head with a reed and spat on him; and they went down on their knees to do him homage. And when they had finished making fun of him, they took off the purple and dressed him in his own clothes (15:16-20).

The passers-by, the chief priests, the scribes and elders all mock Jesus, urge him to come down from the cross and taunt him with the claim that he is the Christ, the King of Israel (15:29-32).

Jesus' last words in Mark are the quotation from Psalm 22, 'My God, my God, why have you deserted me?' (15:34). He is fully human. He 'gave a loud cry and breathed his last' (15:37). It is the centurion who sums up the Gospel claims, 'In truth this man was a son of God' (15:39).

The original Gospel ends with the empty tomb and the women being asked to tell the disciples and Peter that they would see him in Galilee (16:1-8).

In the epilogue to the original Gospel, Jesus appears as he does in other Gospels, with even a reference to his showing himself 'under another form to two of them as they were on their way into the country'(16:12-13). Jesus' final words, before 'his being taken up to the right hand of God' (16:19) are reminiscent of his words at the end of Matthew's Gospel, an exhortation to preach to the whole world. But there is still the Markan touch in Jesus' enumeration of the signs that would accompany the preaching:

> In my name they will cast out devils; they will have the gift of tongues; they will pick up snakes in their hands, and be unharmed should they drink deadly poison; they will lay their hands on the sick who will recover (16:17-18).

And that is the end of the Good News about Jesus Christ, the Son of God, according to Mark.

Luke's Jesus

From the time that Jesus was twelve and stayed behind in the Temple to discuss questions with the elders until his resurrection appearances, especially to the two disciples on the road to Emmaus, the Jesus in Luke's Gospel is meeting people and talking with them. Luke's is a very sociable Jesus. It is not at all difficult to see him as a 'Feeling Jesus'.

Obviously, Jesus, in Luke, can be very objective and justice oriented (especially in criticising the scribes and Pharisees). But, overall, he is sociable, compassionate.

It is only in Luke that we have some description of Jesus' boyhood. In Matthew's Gospel, he is born, is worshipped by the Magi, escapes Herod's massacre by flight into Egypt and goes back to Nazareth. There is a brief portrait of Mary and Joseph, more, in fact, of Joseph from whom Jesus gains his right to be considered a son of David.

On the other hand, Luke sets out to give a portrait of Jesus as a hero, picking and choosing events that enhance the portrait. We listen to long narratives about Zechariah and his wife, Mary's cousin, Elizabeth, her unexpectedly marvellous pregnancy and the birth of John. We listen to long narratives about Mary, including a visit to Elizabeth, her unexpectedly marvellous pregnancy and the wonders and lowliness of Jesus' birth and the events in the stable at Bethlehem.

Both Mary and Zechariah burst into psalm-like personal testimony and song in appreciation of the wonders they have experienced.

This tone continues in Jesus' childhood, from the early days of circumcision and presentation in the Temple to his

Bar Mitzvah days. His first words in the record are, 'Why were you looking for me? Did you not know that I must be busy with my Father's affairs?' A precocious child of great religious ability. But he goes back to Nazareth where he grew up in wisdom, stature and in favour with God and with everyone.

Before he starts on his ministry, we have stories and images of Jesus.

Luke also builds up a sense of anticipation for the coming of Jesus. There is quite a long description of John the Baptist, his preaching, the questions of those who were repenting, 'What must we do, then?' (3:10). 'A feeling of expectancy had grown among the people, who were beginning to think that John might be the Christ' (3:15-16). So, Jesus arrives, is baptised and Luke includes a genealogy back to Adam (3:23-38).

When he started to teach, Jesus was about thirty years old (3:23).

After the biblical interchange in the temptations in the desert, the first words the adult Jesus utters in this Gospel are in the synagogue at Nazareth. He proclaims a text from the book of Isaiah, 'The Spirit of the Lord has been given to me...' (4:18-19). He tells them the text is being fulfilled even as they listen. The immediate response is one of joy and harmony, 'And he won the approval of all, and they were astonished by the gracious words that came from his lips' (4:20-21). But this did not last long. They react, resent him, taunt him with his origins and, enraged, hustle him out of the town to throw him off the brow of the hill (4:28-30). Jesus, however, goes on his way.

Jesus preaches and also begins his healing ministry. Many of the cures are those related in other Gospels. However, there is the personal touch as he listens to the sympathetic arguments concerning the centurion and his building of the synagogue as a reason for the healing of his servant, in his compassion for the widow at Nain, for the woman with the haemorrhage, his touching the leper and taking the hand of the daughter of Jairus.

But one of the main features of the Jesus of Luke is his storytelling. With Matthew and Mark there is little, if any, context given for the parables that Jesus relates. On the other hand, in Luke there is a context and an indication of the personal feelings of Jesus as he tells the story.

The parable of the Good Samaritan (10:29-37) is Jesus' response to some needling by a lawyer who wanted to disconcert him by asking tricky questions. When Jesus responded by questioning him about his understanding of the law, he was anxious to justify himself and wanted to know who was his neighbour. And, when Jesus has told the story, including a few provocative jabs at his listeners because of the behaviour of the priest and the Levite, he gets the lawyer to admit out loud who the neighbour was. Jesus does not congratulate him on giving the correct answer but tells him to go and do the same himself.

The comic-style parable of the unjust judge and the persistent widow (with its message of pestering God for what we want) also has its own introduction. It is about the need to pray continually and never give up (18:1-8) and is followed by another parable about prayer, spoken to some people who prided themselves on being virtuous and despised everyone else, the Pharisee and the publican (18:9-14). With the Pharisee as the villain, it is easy to see Jesus' feeling at the treatment he had received from them.

The Lukan community collected a number of sayings of Jesus about money, introducing them with a parable, that of the crafty steward who gets clients to alter their accounts so that they will welcome him when he is sacked, and ending with a parable, that of the rich man who dined lavishly and the poor man who sat at his gate, neglected (ch. 16).

But the best known parable, that of the lost son, and its introductory parables, the lost sheep and the lost coin, have a significant introduction. It is often said that we do not have as much contact with the actual Jesus of Nazareth as we would like. But these introductions to the parables give us a feel for Jesus and what he was experiencing. The religious leaders had him under constant criticism and attack, especially for his attitudes towards tax collectors and prostitutes. He welcomed them and dined with them. Luke recounts this (15:1-3) and adds 'the Pharisees and the scribes complained'. In response to these complaints, Luke says 'So...' (and there is a lot of feeling in this 'so') '... Jesus spoke this parable to them', to the complaining scribes and Pharisees. The portrait of the two sons and their 'prodigal father' becomes a heartfelt allegory for God and God's dealings with the self-confessed virtuous and sinners.

In this parable, Jesus, the supreme storyteller with his characters' challenging behaviour, the subversive detail in the narrative and the psychological insight into callow selfishness and into repressed envy, tells us about his own experience of God. Jesus, son of Abba, his father, finds human words and emotions in story to communicate to us what God is really like. God is a permissive, loving and lavish father to both sons. We have Jesus' word for it.

Many of Jesus' encounters with people serve as living parables. The episode of the woman who was a sinner in the city (7:36-50) is an embodiment of the parable of the lost son. Here is the woman who has become disillusioned with her life and comes to her senses and realises that she must come back and confess her sinfulness. Jesus, like his father, welcomes her back with lavish love and forgiveness (while the chorus of Simon and his righteous guests complain).

The pleasantly quaint story of short Zacchaeus literally going out on a limb to get a glimpse of Jesus is the same story with the same criticisms and the same results (19:1-10).

Jesus' visit to his friends, Martha and Mary (10:38-42), is just one of many examples of what some have referred to as Jesus' dining ministry in Luke's Gospel. But it also serves as something of a reverse parable of the Good Samaritan. Martha has taken the serving of others to extremes and is 'distracted with all the serving'. Jesus reminds her that in order to love neighbour, one must love God and listen to God's word and discern it, just as Mary did as she sat at his feet like a disciple.

Martha and Mary are two of the many women in the pages of Luke's Gospel. From Mary, the mother of Jesus, to such women as the widow of Nain, the sinner who anointed Jesus, the comforters on the way to Calvary, the group of women who ministered to Jesus, witnessed the crucifixion, went to the tomb and were commissioned to announce that Jesus was risen, there is a strong presence of women in the Gospel.

Luke's version of the passion has most events in common with the other Gospels. However, it amplifies many of the episodes. At the last supper, while there is talk of Judas' betrayal and of Peter's denial of Jesus, there is also conversation about what true greatness is. It is serving exemplified in John's Gospel by the washing of the feet. Peter, then, will learn this attitude of service by his denials and weeping repentance. He will then be in a position to confirm and strengthen his brothers (22:21-34).

Matthew and Mark have Peter remember Jesus' prophetic words about his denial, and then he weeps. Luke adds some detail, 'At that instant, while he was still speaking, the cock crew, and the Lord turned and looked straight at Peter, and Peter remembered what the Lord had said to him...' (22:61-62). And he went outside and wept bitterly.

Three other encounters are exclusive to Luke's passion:

Herod (23:8-12), the women on the way to Calvary (23:26-32), the good thief (23:39-43). Each of these encounters gives a more vivid and personal picture of Jesus as he goes to his death. He is mocked by Herod. He consoles the women who are sad for him, warning them to take care when the difficult days come. And he promises heaven to the good thief who acknowledges his guilt but proclaims the innocence of Jesus.

Matthew and Mark have Jesus express his abandonment as he dies. Instead, Luke has Jesus say, 'Father, into your hands I commend my spirit' (23:46).

The resurrection narratives are made more personal by the long story of the disciples on the road to Emmaus and Jesus opening the eyes of his disciples to the meaning of the Scriptures (and their hearts burning within them as he spoke). The Gospel concludes with the understanding of who Jesus is and what the disciples' mission is: the Christ would suffer but rise from the dead and, in his name, repentance for the forgiveness of sins would be preached to the nations (24:44-48).

Jesus' final words in the Gospel are, 'And now I am sending down to you what the Father has promised. Stay in the city then, until you are clothed with power from on high' (24:49).

But the final gesture from Jesus as he goes to the Father is to give them his blessing (24:50-51). Luke's Jesus is a Jesus who blesses.

John's Jesus

John's Gospel was written at the end of the first century. By this time Jesus has been dead for over fifty years. The early generations of Christians had had time to reflect on the meaning of Jesus' message, his life and his death. In the light of the resurrection, they knew him as the Lord. Further reflection and the facing of controversies about whether Jesus was truly human or not meant that a deepening awareness of Jesus and his humanity and the presence of the divine in him led to the proclamation of Jesus as Word, the Logos who existed before time with the Father and with the Spirit. An understanding of God as Trinity was emerging.

The theology of this Gospel is a High Christology. It is taken for granted in each episode, in each discourse, that Jesus is the Word. This awareness of divinity pervades the presentation of Jesus in his humanity. The portrait of Jesus and the Good News of Jesus communicate, therefore, on many levels.

The portrait of Jesus in John's Gospel can be seen as an Intuitive portrait of an Intuitive Jesus.

The prologue of the Gospel immediately dramatises this in hymn form. The Word, who was with God in the beginning, is God. The Word is also the medium of all creation. The Word brings life to the human race, a life which is light. But the world did not recognise this light, this Word who came to make us all children of God. And this Word was made flesh, lived among us, revealing the glory that belongs to the Word, full of grace and truth (1:1-17).

This is a far cry from the introduction to Jesus in the Synoptic Gospels.

The prologue then introduces Jesus the Christ as the Word:

> Indeed, from his fullness we have, all of us, received
> yes, grace in return for grace,
> since, though the Law was given through Moses.
> Grace and truth have come through Jesus Christ.
> No one has ever seen God;
> it is the only Son, who is nearest to the Father's heart
> who has made him known (1:16-18).

The Johannine community draws on its Greek culture to understand the Word as the Logos. The community also establishes the continuity between Jesus and the Jewish Scriptures and law. And it states the reality of the incarnation, of revelation, of justification, grace and salvation.

In this setting Jesus appears. As in the Synoptics, John, who has been spoken of in the prologue, preaches, baptises Jesus and recognises that he is the beloved servant, pointing him out as the lamb of God (1:19-36; 3:22-36).

While one can build up a human portrait of the human Jesus in John's Gospel, it has to be remembered through every chapter that he is not to be perceived merely as human.

Jesus first invites John's followers to come and see where he is staying. They go to spend the day with him and are so enthused that they start to spread the good news, from Andrew and John to Peter, from Philip to Nathanael. But they are impressed by an intense Jesus who looks hard at Simon and changes his name to Peter, the rock. He greets Nathanael, praising his integrity, but soon speaks to him of the fulfilment of the prophecies of Daniel about the Son of Man (1:35-51).

Jesus is serious, even sombre. He is not pictured as delighting in the enjoyment of the marriage feast of Cana. He is soon making a whip out of cord and driving the money changers out of the Temple, entering into controversy at once over his right to do such things.

But Jesus is seen mainly in his encounters, in his discussions, with a range of people. The first is the Pharisee, Nicodemus, whom he receives at night but who is so impressed with his discussions about being reborn that he ultimately overcomes his fear and asks Pilate for Jesus' body (chs. 3, 19). The second is the Samaritan woman at the well. She is the exact opposite of Nicodemus: a woman, an enemy, a sinner, a scandal, not well-versed in the Scriptures (ch. 4).

Later there is the official pleading for his son's life (ch. 4) and the man who has waited thirty-eight years for a cure at the pool of Bethzatha (ch. 5), who St Augustine speculates symbolically (and intuitively) has appropriately waited thirty-eight years because forty years is the perfect time and he had two bad legs: and two from forty is thirty-eight! There are the woman taken in adultery (ch. 8), the man born blind and his parents (ch. 9), Martha, Mary and Lazarus (ch. 11). The disciples are always there. So, too, are his adversaries, referred to in the Gospel under the generic name, 'the Jews'.

But the encounters are the occasions for Jesus to be believed in. At Cana he lets his glory be seen, and his disciples learned to believe in him (2:11-12). Jesus, the pre-existent Word who became fully human is, therefore, a symbol of God, a 'sacrament' of God's presence on earth. Through his human actions and words, we see more deeply into the person that Jesus is. We are, as Jesus himself did, to go beyond the surface evidence and to see into his heart (2:24-25).

So, Jesus in his encounter with the woman of Samaria, an encounter that is both engaging and challenging to her, to his questioning and somewhat scandalised disciples and to the people of Sychar, is ultimately to be seen as 'living water', the water of creation, the Spirit-filled water of the new heart of Ezekiel (Ezek 36:24-28) which flows from him, when he is seen as the new Temple, in abundance (Ezek 47). This image is repeated in 7:37-39 where the water is once again filled with the Spirit. This culminates in the image of Jesus, pierced on the cross, with blood and water flowing out from his side (19:34).

In the feeding of the thousands and the profound reflection on this new food, transcending the manna in the desert, but which is beyond the comprehension of his listeners with their mundane literalism, he is to be seen as 'the bread of life'.

When the man born blind is pointed out to him and the disciples ask the obtuse question about who was to blame for his affliction, the man himself or his sinful parents, Jesus takes the occasion to proclaim himself 'the light of the world' (9:4-5).

He is the living water, the bread of life, the light of the world.

In the following chapter (10), he gives his principal parable in John's Gospel and identifies himself as the gate of the sheepfold where those who enter will be safe and go freely in and out (v. 9). But it emerges from this chapter, again with reference to Ezekiel (ch. 34), that he is 'the good shepherd'.

He is the living water, the bread of life, the light of the world, the good shepherd – and the resurrection.

While the story of the raising of Lazarus from the dead has its poignant moments as Jesus delays going to heal Lazarus and the disciples are puzzled, as Martha hurries to meet him and laments her brother's death, as Mary quietly grieves and Jesus is moved to tears, we are to see Jesus as the resurrection, the fullness of life (11:25-26).

This is reinforced by the presentation of Jesus as discourser. The bulk of the Gospel is discourse, profound meditations on God's love for the world, redemption and eternal life as well as deeper contemplations of Jesus divine, one with the Father, with whom he sends their Spirit to grace, forgive and enlighten.

Jesus uses the declaration, 'I am' throughout the Gospel. He identifies himself with the Father. The images of water, bread, light, resurrection are symbolic ways of recognising and appreciating this oneness with the Father. Jesus says that he will be fully recognised at the special hour of his exodus, where, like the healing serpents in the desert, he will be lifted up and draw all people to himself. This being lifted up is his crucifixion. It is his hour of glory, of showing to the world the Father's glory. And, as he dies, uttering his complete yes to the Father, he breathes out his Spirit.

Jesus has laid down his life for his friends. That is his new commandment, symbolised by his washing his disciples' feet, to love one another as he has loved us, even to the laying down of life. This is, for us, entering into eternal life and into the mystery of Jesus' oneness with the Father.

This is not easy for the disciple. Judas betrays Jesus. Peter denies him. The apostles flee. Thomas doubts him. Even though Jesus goes with his disciples to Gethsemane in John's Gospel, there is no account of an agony in the garden. However, there is a key incident in John 12:23-33, after Jesus has likened himself to the grain of wheat that must die in the ground before it can yield a rich harvest. Jesus says that he is troubled:

> What shall I say:
> Father, save me from this hour?
> But it was for this very reason that I have come
> to this hour.
> Father, glorify your name.
> A voice came from heaven, 'I have glorified it,
> and will glorify it again'.

It has been suggested that at this moment, the Jesus who

is presented as knowing that he is one with the Father, experiences an alienation from God. Instead of 'I am', it is 'Am I?' This is the agony of the garden in the Synoptic Gospels, God in Jesus experiencing the human abandonment by God.

It is something of this experience that leads us to the end of the original Gospel, through all the passion, 'Behold the man' to Jesus' death, 'He breathed forth his spirit' to the resurrection, 'Tell them I am ascending to my Father and your Father, to my God and your God'. Thomas doubts. Jesus invites him to touch him, to know that it is Jesus, the Word made flesh who is still flesh as Risen Lord.

Jesus' final words in the original Gospel of John are for us as disciples, who do not have the sensate luxury of seeing, hearing and touching Jesus, but who must follow intuitively, in faith:

> You believe because you can see me.
> Happy are those who have not seen and yet believe (20:29).

Gospels and Temperament

Many practitioners of Myers Briggs also use Temperament Theory, especially as developed by David Keirsey and his followers. There is a link with Type because of the ability to categorise the Temperaments with Type letters.

The Temperament that honours continuity and tradition and values, 'The Custodian', can be generally described by the letters SJ, the various combinations (ISTJ, ESTJ, ISFJ, ESFJ) of sensing and judging. On the other hand, the letters SP and its various combinations (ISTP, ESTP, ISFP, ESFP) of sensing and perceiving, indicate a much less rigorously traditional temperament, a freer approach, 'The Artisan'.

Two of the Temperaments can be described with reference to intuition. The various combinations of intuition and feeling (INFJ, INFP, ENFP, ENFJ) denote a temperament that thrives on hunches and possibilities combined with a personalised, subjective approach to action. This is called 'The Idealist', whereas 'The Visionary' is used for the various combinations of intuition and thinking (INTJ, INTP, ENTP, ENTJ), possibilities backed by objectivity: what could be as different from the Idealist's what might be, or wouldn't it be wonderful if...

It has been suggested that if we look at the Gospels in the light of Type, we can be led to an appreciation of them in the light of Temperament. If Matthew's is the Thinking Function Gospel, it is the best candidate for the Custodian, SJ, Gospel. In a similar way, if Mark's is the Sensing Gospel, it is the candidate for the Artisan, SP, Gospel.

Which leaves Luke and John for the Idealist and the Visionary. Luke's portrait of Jesus is the highly personalised portrait, an ideal portrait which relates in Type terms to Feeling (as well as sensation and intuition) but which seems to correspond to the Idealist Temperament (NF). John's Gospel is the Intuitive Gospel and, while much of it offers a personal portrait of Jesus, the Gospel is far more concerned with the vision of Jesus as the Word made flesh who is also one with the Father, which seems to correspond to the Visionary Temperament (NT).

The chapters on each of the Gospels can be read with Temperament in mind. What follows now are some suggestions, rather than detailed treatment, for reading the Gospels according to Temperament.

'The Custodian', SJ and Matthew's Gospel

One of the first things noted about Matthew's community and its Gospel is that it is a Jewish community and that this manifested itself in a concern for the continuity between the early Christian community and its Jewish origins. The traditions were to be preserved as much as possible even if, as is often shown in the Gospel, gentiles from east and west who show faith in Jesus (like the Centurion of chapter 8), will also come into the Church. Jesus of Matthew's Gospel cannot be understood except in this Jewish tradition. He himself says that he did not come 'to abolish the Law or the Prophets but to complete them' (5:17).

The concrete way of showing this continuity and completion of the Law and the Prophets was through the 'Fulfilment Text'. The Gospel is at pains to highlight explicit verses of the Jewish Scriptures and point out how Jesus is the fulfilment of what the texts say. Starting from the genealogy in chapter 1, he is the true Son of David until we reach the Passion narrative where there are quotations from Daniel, Jeremiah, Zechariah, Psalm 22: Jesus is to be seen in the continuity of God's revelation to his people.

The emphasis on the Law is important. In the Infancy Narratives, Jesus is the new Moses. In chapter 5, he goes up the mountain to give a new law to the new covenant people. The Sermon on the Mount is the privileged collection of sayings about the living of the Law that gives credibility to Jesus' continuity with the past. While 'not one dot, not one little stroke shall disappear from the Law until its purpose is achieved' (5:18), Jesus takes the Law on to a higher plane, amplifying what love of God and love of neighbour can mean when his disciples are to be perfect, just as his heavenly father is perfect (5:48). 'So always treat others as you would like them to treat you; that is the meaning of the Law and the Prophets' (6:12).

The impact of Jesus' teaching was profound. What his listeners admired was his 'authority' (7:28-29). Jesus was a man of convictions which were well-grounded in his and their past.

A sense of fairness and justice is also characteristic of the Jesus of Matthew's Gospel (as in the parables which concern money and payment, the unjust steward (18:23-25) and the labourers in the vineyard (20:1-16)) but, once again, Jesus takes the justice on to a higher plane where God's abundant generosity transcends any contractual fairness.

Matthew's Gospel uses the language of the Kingdom of Heaven, the reign of God but it also uses the language of Church. It uses the language of organisation, of structures, of obligations and responsibilities which foreshadows the development of the early Christian communities and assemblies into churches. Tracing the role of Peter through the Gospel gives us an example of how Jesus is seen as preparing for the transition from kingdom to Church. Almost in mid-Gospel, there is the conferral on Peter of the headship and authority of the Church, against which all opposition, the gates of Hell, will not prevail. Peter is the fulfilment of the good steward of the prophecy of Isaiah and receives the keys of the kingdom (Is 22:22). Whatever Peter binds is bound, whatever he looses is loosed in heaven (16:13-19).

And the Gospel concludes with a promise of continuity of which the Church is custodian forever: all authority is given to Jesus by God; he gives it to his apostles; they are to preach his commands, make disciples of the nations and baptise them so that they be recognised as disciples and members of his Church. He pledges his presence until the end of time (28:16-20).

'The Artisan', SP and Mark's Gospel

Mark's Gospel was the first written, the core foundation for the Gospels of Matthew and Luke. It gets on with it. It tells the story of Jesus' ministry as it was preached and remembered in the Markan community. While it has a theological perspective, that Jesus is the Son of God, it does not take the care that Matthew's Gospel does in establishing the continuity with the Jewish Scriptures – it does quote them briefly and they are the pattern for the portrait of Jesus nor does it stylise the portrait of Jesus as a contemporary hero as does Luke – but for Mark, of course, he is – nor does he explore the meditative side of the Gospel as does John. In Mark's Gospel, Jesus acts.

One of the phrases used by commentators earlier in the twentieth century was 'The Messianic Secret'. This was a formula to describe the way the narrative of the Synoptic Gospels, especially Mark's, unfolds. It is a formula to describe the 'low Christology' of the Gospel, the presenting of Jesus as human, gradually revealing to the readers of the Gospel, echoing Jesus' growing understanding of his mission, aspects which later theology would call divinity. In Mark's Gospel, Jesus does not seem to plan the steps of his ministry nor is it suggested that Jesus had any plan, well-thought out or otherwise. In Mark's Gospel, Jesus acts.

He is reticent at first: 'he cast out many devils, but he would not allow them to speak, because they knew who he was' (1:24). He orders the healed leper, 'Mind you say nothing to anyone' (1:44). But Jesus had to learn that he could not impose these restrictions, that people wanted to come to him, that his mission was for all: 'The man (the leper) went away, but then started talking about it freely and telling the story everywhere' (1:45); 'Word went round that he was back; and so many people collected that there was no room left, even in front of the door' (2:2).

And his ministry grows apace. Mark's narratives tend to be brief, focussing on the action: Jesus heals, he confronts the scribes and Pharisees, his relatives are concerned about him, he tells some parables, he calms the storm. From chapter 5 onwards the stories begin to be longer in the telling. Jesus is obviously getting into his stride. He allows people to speak about him. He even urges the Gerasene man who was possessed to spread the news in the Decapolis. He speaks out more confidently against the scribes and Pharisees, sometimes now quoting the Jewish Scriptures.

He is soon moving outside the confines of Galilee and Judaea to preach his Good News. However, he does not manifest the certainty he does in the other Gospels. The profession of faith by Peter has no overtones of Church and authority as it does in Matthew's Gospel. He does not even praise Peter for his acknowledgement that Jesus is the Christ. He just gives 'strict orders not to tell anyone about him' (8:27-30).

He continues his ministry in this manner. Before the last supper and his passion, he spends a whole chapter (ch. 13) in ominous preaching about the final times, an apocalyptic tone that is dramatic and intimidating. Jesus warns that discipleship will not be easy and complacency is alien to his teaching. His last word of advice before the Passover: 'And what I say to you I say to all: Stay awake!' (13:37).

The Passion and Resurrection narratives are brief, each familiar episode told quite succinctly, so much so that the early Church felt the need to give a literary and theological conclusion to the Gospel (16:9-20). In Mark's Gospel, Jesus acts.

'The Idealist', NF and Luke's Gospel

The method and framework of Luke's Gospel contribute to presenting Jesus as hero. He is presented as an ideal. The prologue written to Theophilus (1:1-4) uses the style of ancient Greek and Roman historians to give an account of Jesus, the hero, as a foundation for belief in his teaching.

The carefully constructed and balanced stories of his infancy (the John the Baptist annunciation and birth contrasting with Jesus' annunciation and birth), the poetic allusions to the Jewish Scriptures (more than the use of explicit fulfilment texts), the portrait of Jesus and his mother, all contribute to an introduction to Jesus different from that of the other Gospels. He is the Son of God. He is the graced child of the Law. He is the Jewish boy become adult who is dedicated to God. He is the ideal son who returns to Nazareth, who 'grew in maturity' (2:40), as did his cousin John (1:80), but he also 'increased in wisdom, stature, and in favour with God and all' (2:52).

When Jesus begins his public ministry Luke's Gospel does use a fulfilment text. He is back in Nazareth, is in the synagogue and is invited to read from the scroll of Isaiah. The text is Isaiah 61:1-2, 'The Spirit of the Lord is upon me...'. It is a portrait of the ideal prophet, called and blessed by the Lord, sent in a mission of liberation to the poor and oppressed. And he says, 'This text is being fulfilled this day even as you listen' (4:22).

While Luke's Gospel also has its 'Messianic Secret' perspective, it sometimes does not hesitate to refer to Jesus with his resurrection title, 'Lord'. In his compassion for the widow of Nain, 'The Lord saw her and felt sorry for her...' (7:13). Martha, worrying and fretting about her meal and Mary sitting at Jesus' feet like a male disciple, calls Jesus 'Lord' (10:40).

One of the striking features of Luke's Gospel is Jesus' ability to tell stories, many of them exclusive to this Gospel. While Matthew has Jesus speak a collection of parables at one sitting, Luke often gives a context for these stories. The parables express the feelings of Jesus, his eagerness to encourage those who were losing heart in prayer (18:1), his irritation at those 'who prided themselves on being virtuous and despised everyone else' (18:9), his dismay at the scribes and Pharisees who complained about his eating with tax collectors and prostitutes (15:3).

The parables also offer us insights into God, the God experienced by Jesus who finds human words that can communicate what God is like. God is compassionate, a heart easily moved by the plight of the beaten victim on the road to Jericho, by the sorrow of a wastrel son, by a financial extortioner lowering his eyes in self-effacing prayer in the temple. Luke's Jesus tells us what God is like in the most human of terms.

Jesus related well to a variety of men and a variety of women. He liked people, communicated with them, loved them. Even in his passion, there are these ideal touches as he speaks to the weeping women on the way to Calvary, as he promises paradise to the thief on the cross, even his turning and 'looking straight at Peter' after his denials (and he is referred to here as 'the Lord'), with Peter touched and going outside, weeping bitterly (22:61-62).

And how better to communicate the experience of the Risen Lord than by telling the story of the disciples on the road to Emmaus, drawing out of them their disappointment and thwarted hopes, explaining the Scriptures to them so that their hearts burned within them on the road, breaking bread with them and revealing himself to them (24:13-35)?

The Jesus of Luke's Gospel is a stirring, divinely human Jesus.

'The Visionary', NT and John's Gospel

The Johannine writings have long been called 'visionary': the Gospel, the three Letters and, of course, the visionary book of the Bible par excellence, the Apocalypse, the Book of Revelation and symbolic visions.

What is the vision of John's Gospel?

It begins with a vision of God in eternity, the eternal Logos with God and the Logos becoming incarnate. Light gradually dawns and John, the precursor, announces this light. But he was not heard. Yet, the Logos was made flesh and dwelt among us; the Son, who is nearest to the Father's heart, has made known his glory. The Law came through Moses. Grace and truth now come through Jesus Christ. And this vision of Jesus, this 'high Christology' permeates the whole Gospel.

Even the narratives are referred to as 'signs and wonders'. They are not stories of Jesus in action as in Mark's Gospel. When he performs the signs and those around him are lost in wonder, the Gospel tells us that 'he let his glory be seen'. The Gospel is the gradual manifestation of his glory and the glory of the Father. 'And his disciples believed in him.' Whether it is changing water into wine, raising the official's son to life, curing the man born blind or telling Lazarus to come out of the tomb, these are all indications of glory yet to be revealed. They are invitations to faith.

These signs are also revealed within the context of some stories. However, the stories are the occasion for introducing significant characters who give a tone for the revelation: Mary, Jesus' mother, telling him they have no wine leads him into anticipating his 'hour' (when she will be standing at the foot of his cross) in the setting of marriage, feasting, water and wine; at the well, a sinful woman from a hostile people leads Jesus into a revelation of his sign of living water; eager crowds bountifully fed and wanting him to be king lead him to the revelation of his sign of the bread of life; the man born blind through no fault of his own leads him into the sign of light, the light of the world; Martha, saddened at Lazarus' death leads him into the sign of resurrection, life after death. They are all part of the Glory of Jesus and the Father.

The vision in John's Gospel is mystical. Jesus acts but he also reflects and prays, his discourses are mystical prayer attempting to express in limited, human words, his relationship to the father and the nature of the incarnation and his mission. He joins this prayer with the signs of his glory in the Exodus name of God, 'I am'. He says that he manifests the Father as 'I am the living water', 'I am the bread of life', 'I am the light of the world', 'I am the Good Shepherd', 'I am the resurrection and the life'.

The figure of Jesus on the cross is the completion of this revelation. It is 'the hour' of his passing from this world to his Father, his exodus, as he, the finest Paschal lamb is lifted up on the cross, drawing all people to himself. Then all know that 'I am he'. The suffering Jesus is glorious on the Cross and breathes forth the Spirit. It is finished. It is finished for Jesus as blood and water, symbols of life and life-giving flow from his side. But it is not finished for his disciples. Life after death, the resurrection, is a sign, a wonder, of glory. Therefore Jesus is the Risen Lord.

This is John's vision of Jesus. But the Gospel is also anchored in the reality of those who come after Jesus, who are more blessed because they do not see. It is in the symbolic picture of Thomas in the upper room with his doubts which sets the scene for vision to come down to earth. Thomas, at the invitation of Jesus, 'doubt no longer, but believe', touches, physically touches, the wounds in the hands and side of Jesus.

'My Lord and my God.'

Finally

This journey through the Gospels has been an attempt to see Jesus and the Good News through a new and a particular perspective, that of Type, especially as derived from Carl G. Jung and developed by Isabel Myers and her mother, Katharine Briggs. The early Christian communities seem to have responded to Jesus as all things to all people. Every person of every Type can find enough of Jesus' words and actions to elicit a personal response. And there is enough to challenge each of us in our opposite Functions so that, without our own efforts but by answering to God's grace, we can grow.

The twentieth century art form, the movies, offers us a range of images and narratives, some of which appeal, some of which do not, according to our Type preferences. They are a readily available resource – and an interesting and entertaining resource at that.

Just as I was about to conclude this journey I found a page that I had put aside a year earlier and had forgotten. It was one of those pages of schematic material designed for teachers or seminar leaders and its subject was Jesus (*Information Bulletin, No.26, August 1997, Commission for the Continuing Education of Priests*). The schema that it set out for Jesus and the four Gospels rather appealed to me and seems to be an appropriate way to finish the book.

Mark	*Matthew*	*Luke*	*John*
the	*the*	*the*	*the*
Storyteller	*Theologian*	*Word Artist*	*Mystagogue*
Son of Man	Teacher	Saviour	Word
who is	of God's	of	of
Son of God	New Covenant	the poor	hidden God
Discipleship	*Kingdom*	*Salvation*	*Eternal Life*

Appendix:
The Myers Briggs Type Indicator

In an age of psychology and self-awareness, especially in the Western world, there are many theories, many experiences, many techniques that help us towards better intra-communication (understanding of what is going on *within* us) and better inter-communication (understanding what is going on *between* us).

In the late nineteenth century and early twentieth century (the era of the development of psychology), writers such as Sigmund Freud and Carl Jung in Europe alerted the world to facets of the human psyche and human behaviour that were known but not appreciated, or whose implications were not realised. Psychology uses the data of experience when formulating theories and hypotheses. Needless to say, not all of these are verified. But enough research and reflection has gone on to make many findings of psychology respectable – and even indispensable.

The Myers Briggs Type Indicator looks at a particular way of considering human behaviour and the processes that lie behind our behaviour. It is, of course not meant to be *the* explanation of the way we act. Rather, it considers the ways we function: the ways in which we perceive our world, the ways in which we come to grips with it in action.

In the early decades of the twentieth century, American Katharine Briggs, an avid student of human nature and a woman of great insight, found that Carl Jung had formulated categories to describe human behaviour and processes that expressed well what she had discovered. Her daughter, Isabel Myers, spent several decades before her death in 1980, developing theories that she and her mother had worked on, along with observations, statistical data and conclusions of her own. After considerable time and testing, she produced a questionnaire designed to gauge the way individuals function. The questionnaire (which has undergone further verification for reliability and validity over several years and which has developed into several more sophisticated forms) is an *indicator* of preferred ways of functioning.

With its basis firmly in Jung's descriptions, and its acknowledgement that there are no right and wrong ways of functioning but simply differences, the indicator (MBTI) has become very popular in the United States and, by now, all around the world.

Individuals have found that the results and the explanations offered have affirmed as well as challenged them. Groups in business management, school staffs, nursing staffs and religious communities have used the results to appreciate differences in point of view and to foster communication rather than continue with past frustrations.

The main focal points of the MBTI are:

1. The sources of our energy – from within or from the world outside us: the question of introversion and extraversion.

2. The ways we perceive reality, either in present concrete detail sensately or by appreciating hunches and possibilities intuitively.

3. The ways we act, either thinking clearly logically or, in a more subjective way, basing our decisions on our personal values before logic – feeling.

4. The way we act in the outer world whether we are introverts or extraverts: our propensity for decisiveness, and judging, or for keeping our options open and data-gathering, perceiving.

The symbols used are:

- **E** for Extraversion
- **I** for Introversion
- **S** for Sensation
- **N** for Intuition
- **T** for Thinking
- **F** for Feeling
- **J** for Judging
- **P** for Perceiving.

Jung observed that people show a preference for the world in which they operate best. The preference could be slight or marked. And, of course, the strength of the preference varies at different times of our lives, let alone at different times of the day. But it is a preference nonetheless. This ordinary human behaviour and the natural preference cannot be labelled right or wrong and neither is better than the other. This is a good and important caution.

Extraversion, in the way Jung and his interpreters have used the word, means an attitude by which a person prefers the outer world of people and things to their own inner world. It is where they draw their energy from, the world they look to when they need replenishment. Introversion can be very draining.

Introverts, Jung would say, are those who are more comfortable in their own inner world of ideas, feelings and imagination. They draw their energy and their replenishment from within. Extraversion can be very draining.

Jung also noted how people perceived their world. At their extremes, our ways of noticing tend toward opposite poles although we are able to and do function in both ways. It is just that one is more congenial and comfortable.

Basically, sensing indicates awareness through the five senses. This way of perceiving anchors us in reality, the reality of the outer world as well as the reality of our inner world. The great qualities of this way of functioning are attentiveness, a strong sense of presence, awareness of detail, of time and space and, though we are all prone to untidiness, a sense of order. If we are sensate people, we take it for granted that we are down to earth, and realistic.

But there are other people who are not such 'feet on the ground' types. They are definitely 'up in the air'. They are hardly realistic – at least, not all the time. They overlook detail, often not noticing it until it is pointed out by the eager sensate. They are intuitive. The great qualities of this way of functioning seem to do with leaps of understanding, capacity for making links and associations between seemingly disparate realities, sixth sense vibes and hunches.

Jung noted that we go into action in either of two ways. They appear to be contraries. However, each of us uses both. We are simply more comfortable with one way than with the other.

Here the two preferred ways of functioning are thinking and feeling. The thinking function means that we go into action on the basis of principle, order, clear thinking, logic and consequences. The thinking function enables us to make decisions that are part of our integrity. Thinkers aim for objectivity. This sounds somewhat impersonal and it is.

The feeling function has an inbuilt difficulty in its name. Jung was not referring to feeling in its emotional sense. It is true to say that many thinkers can be quite impassioned (feeling, emotional) in their stances on principle. Some feelers may seem far less emotional in their personalised decisions, 'cool', more phlegmatic in manner.

The feeling function responds to values rather than to logic. Its preference is for more varied factors to be introduced into decision-making: circumstances, the need for harmony. Feelers include more subjective elements in their decisions and actions.

These ways of deciding and acting are not necessarily opposed. They both offer rational criteria for decisions. In fact, they are complementary. The thinker's strength is in the affirmation of principle (where the feeler might be too caught up in a personalised view of the matter). The feeler's strength is in the nuances of a situation that might require more attention and appreciation (where the thinker might ride roughshod over people for the sake of truth).

It was not so much Jung but scholars following his lead who highlighted the contrast between the attitudes of judging and perceiving. Isabel Myers brought these attitudes to clear focus and incorporated them into her Type Indicator. Both deal with how we act in the outer world.

The first is the attitude that wants to get the show on the road. The second wants to gather more data before the show gets on the road. The former often appears decisive, the latter indecisive. The first is judging. However, judging does not signify being critically judgmental. Rather, it is to be understood as the propensity for making judgements and putting them into action. The second is perceiving. This does not mean that a person is necessarily perceptive in the sense that he or she has great sensitivity towards people. Rather, it means that the person is open to more and more data.

The great strength of judging is that decisions are congenial and get made. The great strength of perceiving is that more detail becomes available for a more comprehensive decision or more creative insights are offered for a wider range of decisions.

Clearly no one acts out in a textbook fashion the attitudes and functions that have been described. The descriptions (better than 'labels' which has overtones of glib titles and narrow interpretation) are helpful in naming facets of our processes and behaviour and encouraging us to explore them further.

The MBTI highlights the sixteen possible combinations that result:

There are four Types which are comfortable with Sensate Thinking Functioning:
ISTJ
ISTP
ESTP
ESTJ

There are four Types which are comfortable with Sensate Feeling Functioning:
ISFJ
ISFP
ESFP
ESFJ

There are four Types which are comfortable with Intuitive Feeling Functioning:
INFJ
INFP
ENFP
ENFJ

There are four Types which are comfortable with Intuitive Thinking Functioning:
INTJ
INTP
ENTP
ENTJ

Further insight into the Indicator, which is beyond the scope of this book, can be gained from looking at the preferences of each of the sixteen types in terms of the four functions: sensing, intuition, thinking, feeling. As has been said, we exercise all four but are more comfortable with one than with another. Theory suggests that we have a most preferred function, probably developed personally but unselfconsciously during our early years. The literature refers to this most favoured function as the Dominant Function.

As we grow, especially in our formative adolescent years, another function is also developed and is used congenially and in association with the Dominant. This second function is called the Auxiliary Function. Thus, a dominantly sensate person could have as Auxiliary either thinking or feeling. A dominantly feeling person could have as Auxiliary either sensing or intuition. And so on.

As life goes on, we are challenged (and should challenge ourselves) to develop the less congenial and utilised functions. The opposite to the Auxiliary function is called the Tertiary. It is suggested that this function comes into play as we enter adult life and want a new challenge. Our Dominant and Auxiliary can always be relied on. But now is the time for moving towards greater wholeness.

The fourth function, the one least developed, even frequently ignored (except when we are not ourselves and it tends to assert itself without our wanting it to), is, of course, the opposite to our Dominant Function. It has been named our Inferior Function. Many agree that it is a lifetime's challenge to work on and with this Inferior Function.

Dominant Thinkers are so at home with objectivity that they neglect Feeling. Feelers are so caught up in their personalised world that they have not developed the objective approach to decision-making. Sensates are so anchored to the present that possibilities can be alarming. Intuitives are so caught up with what might be that they overlook and miss out on what actually is.

This has been an 'introduction' to some of the basic ideas, based on Jung, and developed by Katharine Briggs and Isabel Myers. There is a great deal more to be said, a great deal that is illuminating for our life's journey.

[This material on the Myers Briggs Type Indicator has been abridged from the introduction to Peter Malone, *Let a Viking Do It*, Hagar and Family Illustrate the Myers Briggs Type Indicator (David Lovell, Melbourne, 1996).]

Bibliography

Dwyer, Margaret, *No Light without Shadow*, Melbourne, Desbooks, 1997.

Grant, W. Harold; Thompson, Magdala; Clarke, Thomas E., *From Image to Likeness: A Jungian Path in the Gospel Journey*, New York/Ramsay, Paulist Press, 1983.

Francis, Leslie J., *Personality Type and Scripture: Exploring Mark's Gospel,* London, Mowbray, 1997.

Michael, C.P. and Morrissey, M.C., *Prayer and Temperament*, Charlottesville, The Open Book Inc.

Richardson, P.T., *Four Spiritualities: Expressions of Self; Expressions of Spirit*, Palo Alto, Davies-Black, 1996.

Sanford, John, *The Kingdom Within: A Study of the Inner Meaning of Jesus' Sayings*, Philadelphia, Lippincott, 1970.